DIAMONDS

Books by Antoinette Matlins
(all GemStone Press)

COLORED GEMSTONES: THE ANTOINETTE MATLINS BUYING GUIDE
How to Select, Buy, Care for & Enjoy Sapphires, Emeralds, Rubies
and Other Colored Gems with Confidence and Knowledge

THE PEARL BOOK: THE DEFINITIVE BUYING GUIDE
How to Select, Buy, Care for & Enjoy Pearls
2nd edition

JEWELRY & GEMS: THE BUYING GUIDE
How to Buy Diamonds, Pearls, Colored Gemstones, Gold & Jewelry
with Confidence and Knowledge
5th edition

GEM IDENTIFICATION MADE EASY
A Hands-On Guide to More Confident Buying & Selling
2nd edition

ENGAGEMENT & WEDDING RINGS
The Definitive Buying Guide for People in Love
2nd edition

JEWELRY & GEMS AT AUCTION
The Definitive Guide to Buying & Selling at the Auction House
& on Internet Auction Sites

DIAMONDS

The Antoinette Matlins Buying Guide

How to Select, Buy, Care for & Enjoy Diamonds with Confidence and Knowledge

Antoinette Matlins, P.G.

GEMSTONE PRESS
Woodstock, Vermont

Diamonds
The Antoinette Matlins Buying Guide

2002 Second Printing
2001 First Printing
© 2001 by Antoinette L. Matlins

For information regarding permission to reprint material from this book, please mail or fax your request in writing to GemStone Press, Permissions Department, at the address / fax number listed below.

Library of Congress Cataloging-in-Publication Data

Matlins, Antoinette Leonard.
Diamonds—the Antoinette Matlins buying guide : how to select, buy, care for & enjoy diamonds with confidence and knowledge / Antoinette L. Matlins
      p. cm.
Includes bibliographical references and index.
ISBN 0-943763-32-0
1. Diamonds. I. Title: Diamonds. II. Title: Antoinette Matlins buying guide.
III. Title.
TS753 .M38 2001
553.8'2—dc21

2001003692

10   9   8   7   6   5   4   3   2
Manufactured in the United States of America

Cover Design: Stacey Hood
Interior Design: Chelsea Cloeter
Color Insert: Bridgett Taylor

GemStone Press
A Division of LongHill Partners, Inc.
Sunset Farm Offices, Route 4, P.O. Box 237
Woodstock, VT 05091
Tel: (802) 457-4000   Fax: (802) 457-4004
www.gemstonepress.com

Contents

PART ONE Appreciating Diamonds

PART TWO Diamonds

PART THREE

Design & Style: Getting the Look You Want

Color Photograph Section

Acknowledgments

There are many people who have helped me learn and understand the complexities of this exciting field—too many to try to mention all of them here. Nonetheless, there are a few people who have been especially influential and supportive of the work I have done, and I would like to take a moment to acknowledge them. In addition to my father, I would like to thank my brother Kenneth Bonanno, F.G.A., P.G., and my sisters Karen Bonanno DeHaas, F.G.A., P.G., and Kathryn Bonanno Patrizzi, F.G.A., P.G., from whom I continue to learn, and with whom I enjoy sharing and debating gemological issues. I would also like to thank, in particular, C.R. "Cap" Beesley, Director of American Gemological Laboratories, New York; he has been a great teacher, and his research and leadership have benefited the entire gem and jewelry community.

I would also like to thank Robert Crowningshield, Vice President of Identification Services, Gemological Institute of America (GIA) Gem Trade Laboratory. A wonderful friend to my father, he has always been generous in the time he has given me to address questions or issues I might have. Mr. Crowningshield's work for the past half-century in the field of diamonds and gemstones, and his contributions to the gemological literature, have helped shape the world of gemology as we know it.

At GemStone Press I would like to thank Sandra Korinchak, Polly Mahoney, and Bridgett Taylor, with whom it has been a pleasure to work, and who have made the project fun.

And last, but not least, I want to thank my husband, Stuart Matlins, for his unfailing support and encouragement, and for his willingness to spend many lonely nights while I'm traveling around the world to pursue my work.

Dedication

This book is specially dedicated to my father, Antonio C. Bonanno, who died in 1996. He inspired me as a child and filled my world with awe and wonder. He was my teacher, my mentor, and my coauthor on three books. Although his name is not on this cover, his knowledge and wisdom—his words, his ideas, his values—fill its pages. My gratitude is eternal.

Preface

From the time I was a small child, I had the pleasure of being sur-rounded by beautiful gems and had a unique opportunity to learn the gem business. Having a father who was a well-known gemologist, appraiser, and collector—described as the "father of modern, practical gemology" prior to his death—I was able to spend hours marveling at stones, those in his own private collection as well as those brought to him to be professionally identified and evaluated.

Dinner conversation always centered on the day's events at my father's office. Sometimes he would thrill us with an account of a partic-ularly fine or rare gem he had had the pleasure of identifying or verify-ing. But too often the subject would turn to some poor, unknowing consumer who had been victimized. It might have been a soldier who thought he had purchased genuine diamonds while visiting Africa, and learned sadly that they were inexpensive quartz pebbles; or a housewife who bought a "diamond" ring at an estate sale, only to learn the stone was a colorless zircon or white sapphire. It might have been a doctor who thought he had purchased a rare "canary" color diamond as a gift for his wife, who learned to his dismay that the beautiful bright yellow color was not natural at all but the result of special treatment, so the stone was not worth anywhere near what he had paid for it.

I grew up with a deep appreciation and passion for diamonds, but also with a keen awareness of the pitfalls of the trade. This led to my first book, *Jewelry & Gems: The Buying Guide*—the first book ever writ-ten to help consumers and lay people understand what they were really buying. Now, after five editions and over 250,000 copies—in English, Spanish, Greek, Russian, and Arabic—there have been so many changes in the diamond field that the time has come for a book focused exclu-sively on diamonds.

As with my other books, the purpose of this book is to provide a basic but complete consumer's guide to buying a diamond, whether for your own personal pleasure, as a gift, or as an investment in something beautiful to pass on as a treasured heirloom. It is designed and written for a wide market—for husbands, wives, or parents buying a sparkling gift for a loved one to mark a special moment; for young couples looking for the perfect stone for an engagement ring; for tourists, business travelers, and service men or women hoping to pick up a diamond at a "bargain" price while near the mines or cutting centers; and for collectors and connoisseurs who simply love diamonds and want to know more about them. It is written to give you information you need, in relevant terms you can understand.

In the following pages you will find what you need to know to make wiser choices and avoid costly mistakes. I wish to stress, however, that the purpose is not to give you false confidence, nor is it to frighten you or discourage you from buying diamonds and jewelry with confidence. My primary purpose is to make you less vulnerable to the allure of *bargains* and make you aware of the importance of buying from knowledgeable, reputable jewelers; and to make you a more knowledgeable shopper and help transform a confusing—often frightening—experience into one that is truly interesting, exciting, and safe.

I hope you enjoy *Diamonds: The Antoinette Matlins Buying Guide* and find it to be an indispensable guide. Most of all, I hope it will remove any fear and enable you to experience the wonder, surprise, and romance that should be part of discovering the "perfect" diamond, a special stone that, when you look upon it, will bring the "sparkle" of delight to your eyes!

Antoinette Matlins

Introduction

Throughout history, diamonds have been prized above all other gems. Their beauty, rarity, and inherent "magical powers" have made them the symbol of kings, of power, of wealth, and of love. Every civilization, every society, grandly exhibits its fascination with and desire to possess these sparkling creations. And so it continues to this very day. We are no different from the generations that have come before, and global diamond sales continue to reach new heights.

With each passing year there are new developments in the world of diamonds—stunning new designs, new shapes, and "fancy" colors. Major new diamond deposits have also been discovered in new places, including Colorado and Canada; Canada's Ekati diamond mine is rapidly emerging as a major source of fine quality diamonds. And believe it or not, we even have diamonds that *sing* (see chapter 1)!

But along with all the wonderful new developments come more things to *look out* for, and more reasons *not* to base your choice on price alone:

- **Diamonds are being treated in new ways to alter color**—including high pressure/high temperature methods that transform common tinted diamonds into highly prized colorless gems and exotic "fancy" colors (see chapter 12).
- **New lasering techniques and glasslike fillers** are being used to improve clarity (see chapter 7).
- **Synthetic diamonds** are more common, especially in fancy colors, sometimes erroneously identified and sold as natural gems (see chapter 10).
- **New diamond *imitations* are fooling diamond testers** (see chapter 10).

Adding to the complexity of buying a diamond today is the marketplace itself, and *where* to buy. The retail marketplace is more competitive than ever, with no less than ten jewelry stores in every major mall.

Showrooms claiming to sell to the public at "wholesale" prices are popping up in almost every state. And internet commerce, including online auction sites, has entered the diamond arena!

Diamond Branding Makes Its Debut

In an effort to attract customers and reassure them on matters of reliability, integrity, and the quality of products being offered, many companies are now *branding* what they sell. We find names we recognize and trust—such as De Beers—now selling "De Beers diamonds" directly to consumers. There is certainly name recognition in the De Beers brand, and it also carries with it a reputation for unparalleled expertise in the diamond field; the company hopes the brand identification will instill confidence in consumers to buy their product over another.

Retailers and designers are also getting into the branding act. You will find specially commissioned diamond cuts such as Tiffany's unique *Lucida*™ diamond cut available only at Tiffany, the unique *Noble Cut*™ commissioned on an exclusive basis by designer Doron Isaak for his Couture Gems collection, and the *Escada*® designed exclusively for the famous fashion house. Even diamond *cutters* are branding their product in an effort to reassure consumers that the diamond they are considering exhibits maximum beauty resulting from precision cutting. Currently, some of the best known cutting brands—brands that help assure consumers of precision cutting—include the *Lazare Kaplan Ideal*®, *EightStar*®, *Hearts on Fire*®, *Gabrielle*®, *Context*®, and the *Spirit Sun*®. You will find more on cutting considerations and innovations in chapter 5. Branded diamonds are specially marked so that they can be identified and verified. This is currently done using laser technology to inscribe pertinent information along the diamond's edge—usually the brand name and logo, and a registration number that corresponds with the certificate issued with the diamond.

More and more brands are entering the market, but today most diamonds sold have no brand identification. There are many beautiful diamonds that have no "signature" but are equally dazzling; some may also offer better value. Furthermore, trademarked cuts are already being duplicated with minor alterations, sometimes so closely resembling the original that differences can only be seen with magnification. Keep in mind also that a brand name isn't always a guarantee of quality, especially in the secondary market—estate sales, auctions, pawnshops, and so on. There have already been reports of *faked* brand identification where a respected brand name—complete with logo and number—were laser inscribed on a diamond in order to represent it as a diamond of much better quality. It is relatively easy and inexpensive to laser inscribe diamonds, so we cannot ignore the possibility that the incidence of this type of fraud might increase. New technology may provide a solution; *ion imaging,* for example, offers some promise in this area (see chapter 9).

The future of diamond branding is still unknown. Whether or not consumers will find it helpful or more confusing, only time will tell. But whatever the case, branding is no substitute for knowledge.

Now more than ever, understanding as much as possible about what you are buying is the key to getting what you really want, paying the right price, and enjoying your diamond purchases for years to come. In *Diamonds: The Antoinette Matlins Buying Guide,* you will find the information you need, including:

- The factors affecting quality differences in diamonds.
- Diamond grading reports and how to interpret what the information really means.
- How to compare prices.
- How to spot differences in stones that may *appear* to be the same quality.
- Fraudulent practices to guard against.
- How to protect yourself from misrepresentation.
- Questions to ask when buying any diamond.
- What to get *in writing.*
- How to select a reliable jeweler, appraiser, and insurer.
- How to select the right style and design.
- How to get what you want within your budget.
- …and more.

The experience of buying a diamond doesn't have to be confusing and overwhelming, intimidating, or terrifying. Within the following pages you will find the key to experiencing the magic, excitement, and pleasure.

Antoinette Matlins

PART  ONE

Appreciating Diamonds

CHAPTER ONE

The Magic of Diamonds

The substance that possesses the greatest value, not only among the precious stones, but of all human possessions is the diamond ... which for a long time was known to kings only, and to very few of them.

From the *37th Book of the Historie of the World*, by Roman historian
C. Plinius Secundus, published in the year 77 A.D.

The diamond has been one of the most coveted gems in history. Uncut diamonds adorned the suits of armor of the great knights; cut diamonds have adorned the crowns of kings and queens throughout the ages, and today the diamond is internationally recognized as a symbol of love and betrothal. Diamond, nature's hardest substance—uniquely able to resist both fire and steel, and therefore all of humankind's early efforts to alter it—epitomized unyielding power and invincible strength. It seemed truly indestructible. The word *diamond* comes from the Greek word *adamas* and its Roman equivalent *diamas,* which meant "the unconquerable."

Legends of the diamond's mythical properties have been passed along for centuries. In India, where diamonds were first discovered several thousand years ago, the diamond was valued more for its strength and magic than for its beauty. The diamond was thought to protect its wearer from snakes, fire, poison, illness, thieves, and all the combined forces of evil.

As the gemstone of the zodiac House of Aries, symbolized by the ram, the diamond was believed by ancient astrologers to be powerful for people born under the planet Mars. They thought diamonds could provide fortitude, strength of mind, and continuous love in marriage, as well as ward off witchcraft, poisons, and nightmares.

Each culture has prized the diamond for its unique properties. The Romans believed that a diamond worn against the skin of their left arm would help them remain brave and daring in battle and give them victory over their enemies. An ancient passage reads: "He who carries a diamond on the left side shall be hardy and manly; it will guard him from accidents to the limbs; but nevertheless a good diamond will lose its power and virtue if worn by one who is incontinent, or drunken." Another Roman practice was to set diamonds in steel to serve as a charm against insanity.

The diamond has been credited with many magical powers. At one time it was considered the emblem of fearlessness and invincibility; the mere possession of a diamond would endow the wearer with superior strength, bravery, and courage. It was also believed that a diamond could drive away the devil and all spirits of the night.

During the 1500s, diamonds were looked upon as talismans that could enhance the love of a husband for his wife. In the Talmud, a gem that from its description was probably a diamond was worn by the high priest and served to prove innocence or guilt. If an accused person was guilty, the stone grew dim; if the person was innocent, it shone more brilliantly than ever!

Besides being colorless, diamonds occur in every color of the rainbow. The Hindus classed diamonds according to the four castes. The Brahmin diamond (colorless) gave power, friends, riches, and good luck; the Kshatriya (brown/champagne) prevented old age; Vaisya (the color of a kodali flower) brought success; and the Sudra (a diamond with the sheen of a polished blade—probably gray or black) brought all types of good fortune. Red and yellow diamonds were exclusively royal gems, for kings alone.

Diamonds have been associated with almost everything from producing sleepwalking to producing invincibility and spiritual ecstasy. Even sexual prowess has been strongly attributed to the diamond. There is a catch, however, to all the mythical powers associated with this remarkable gem. One must find the diamond "naturally" in order to experience its magic, for it loses its powers if acquired by purchase. However, when a diamond is offered as a pledge of love or friendship, its potency may return—another good reason for its presence in the engagement ring!

Diamonds to Delight the *Ear* as Well as the Eye

Diamonds are creating a new sensation, quite literally, as they move from the visual realm to the realm of *sound*. Now, in addition to liking the way a diamond looks, you may soon be able to decide if you like the way it sounds!

Advanced technology now makes it possible to translate lightwave patterns into soundwaves—sound that can be consistently reproduced and recorded. Each diamond has a unique pattern that creates a unique sound. This new, patent-pending innovation called *Diamond Melody* was pioneered by Gabi Tolkowsky, world renowned diamond cutter and cousin of Marcel Tolkowsky (father of the modern American ideal cut diamond), and Gemprint, the Canadian company specializing in diamond laser identification.

At a recent conference, Gabi Tolkowsky played a CD that filled the room with a dreamy, abstract sound. There was an almost other-worldly dimension to what we were hearing, random yet beautiful. We then heard another work, this one a clearly different composition, but with the same absorbing, new-age sound. And then we were told who the composers were: two diamonds!

One day in the near future, it may well be possible to go to a jewelry store and select a diamond not only because of its visual characteristics, but because of its unique sound. The diamond of the twenty-first century may do more than dazzle the eye—it may also enchant the ear!

CHAPTER TWO

Becoming Intimate with Diamonds

Diamonds should never be bought as a gamble—the uneducated consumer will always lose. This is a basic rule of thumb. The best way to take the gamble out of buying a particular diamond is to familiarize yourself with the stone. While the average consumer can't hope to make the same precise judgments as a qualified gemologist, whose scientific training and wealth of practical experience provide a far greater database from which to operate, the consumer can learn to judge a stone as a "total personality" and learn what the critical factors are—color, clarity (also referred to in the trade as "perfection"), cut, brilliance, and weight—and how to balance them in judging the diamond's value. Learning about these factors and spending time in the marketplace looking, listening, and asking questions before making the purchase will prepare you to be a wise buyer more likely to get what you really want, at a fair price.

Try to learn as much as you can about the diamond you want to buy. Examine stones owned by your family and friends, and compare stones at several different jewelry stores, noting differences in shades of colors, brilliance, and cut. Go to a good, established jewelry store and ask to see fine stones. If the prices vary, ask why. Let the jeweler point out differences in color, cut, or brilliance, and if he can't, go to another jeweler with greater expertise. Begin to develop an eye for what constitutes a fine stone by looking, listening, and asking good questions.

Here are five key questions to ask yourself initially before you consider buying any stone:

1. Is the color what you desire?
2. Is the shape what you want?

3. Does it have liveliness, or "zip"?
4. Do you like it and feel excited by it?
5. Can you afford it?

If you answer yes to all five questions, you are ready to examine the specific stone more carefully.

The Six Key Steps in Examining a Stone

1. *Whenever possible, examine stones unmounted.* They can be examined more thoroughly out of their settings, and defects cannot be hidden by the mounting or side stones.
2. *Make sure the diamond is clean.* If you are buying a stone from a retail jeweler, ask that it be cleaned for you. If you are not in a place where it can be cleaned professionally, breathe on the stone in a huffing manner in order to steam it with your breath, and then wipe it with a clean handkerchief. This will at least remove the superficial film of grease.
3. *Hold the unmounted stone so that your fingers touch only the girdle* (the edge where top and bottom meet). Putting your fingers on the table (top) and/or pavilion (bottom) will leave traces of oil, which will affect color and brilliance.

   The *careful* use of tweezers instead of fingers is recommended only if you feel comfortable using them. Make sure you know how to use them, and get the permission of the owner before picking up the diamond. It is easy for the stone to pop out of the tweezers and to become damaged or lost, and you could be held responsible.
4. *View the diamond under proper lighting.* Many jewelers use numerous incandescent spotlights, usually recessed in dropped ceilings. Some use special spotlights that can make any stone—even glass imitations—look fantastic.

   Fluorescent lights are what professionals use for diamond grading, but they *adversely* affect the appearance of the stone. Diamonds will not show as much brilliance and fire, as much sparkle, when viewed under fluorescent lighting. I recommend looking at diamonds in several types of light, including daylight when it is available (sometimes the jeweler will let you walk to a window, or go outside, to better see the stone's personality).

The light source should come from above or behind you, shining down and through the stone, so that the light traveling through the stone is reflected back up to your eye.

5. *Rotate the stone in order to view it from different angles.*
6. *If you are using a loupe, focus it both on the surface and into the interior.* To focus into the interior, shift the stone slowly, raising or lowering it, until you focus clearly on all depths within it. This is important because if you focus on the top only, you won't see what is in the interior of the stone.

How to Use a Loupe

A loupe (pronounced *loop*) is a special type of magnifying glass. The loupe can be very helpful in many situations, even for the beginner. With a loupe you can check a stone for chips or scratches or examine certain types of noticeable inclusions more closely. Remember, however, that even with a loupe, you will not have the knowledge or skill to see or under stand the many telltale indicators that an experienced jeweler or gemologist could spot. No book can provide you with that knowledge or skill. Do not allow yourself to be deluded, or let a little knowledge give you a false confidence. Nothing will more quickly alienate a reputable jeweler or mark you faster as easy prey for the disreputable dealer.

The loupe is a very practical tool to use once you master it, and with practice it will become more and more valuable. The correct type is a 10x, or ten-power, "triplet," which can be obtained from any optical supply house. The triplet type is recommended because it corrects two problems other types of magnifiers have: traces of color normally found at the outer edge of the lens, and visual distortion, also usually at the outer edge of the lens. In addition, the loupe must have a black housing around the lens, not chrome or gold, either of which might affect the color you see in the stone.

The loupe *must* be 10x because the United States Federal Trade Commission requires grading to be done under ten-power magnification. Any flaw that does not show up under 10x magnification is considered nonexistent for grading purposes.

With a few minutes' practice you can easily learn to use the loupe. Here's how:

1. Hold the loupe between the thumb and forefinger of either hand.
2. Hold the stone or jewelry similarly in the other hand.
3. Bring both hands together so that the fleshy parts just below the thumbs are pushed together and braced by the lower portion of each hand just above the wrists (the wrist portion is actually a pivot point).
4. Now move both hands up to your nose or cheek, with the loupe as close to your eye as possible. If you wear eyeglasses, you do not have to remove them.
5. Get a steady hand. With diamonds it's very important to have steady hands for careful examination. With your hands still together and braced against your face, put your elbows on a table. (If a table isn't available, brace your arms against your chest or rib cage.) If you do this properly you will have a steady hand.

A 10x Triplet Loupe

How to hold a loupe
when examining a stone

Practice with the loupe, keeping it approximately one inch (more or less) from your eye, and about an inch from the object being examined. Learn to see through it clearly. A 10x loupe is difficult to focus initially, but with a little practice it will become easy. You can practice on any object that is difficult to see—the pores in your skin, a strand of hair, a pinhead, or your own jewelry.

Play with the item being examined. Rotate it slowly, tilt it back and forth while rotating it, and look at it from different angles and different directions. It won't take long before you are able to focus easily on anything you wish to examine. If you aren't sure about your technique, a knowledgeable jeweler will be happy to help you learn to use the loupe correctly.

What the Loupe Can Tell You

With practice and experience (and further education if you're really serious), a loupe can tell even the amateur a great deal. For a gemologist it can help determine whether the stone is natural, synthetic, glass, or doublet (a composite stone to be discussed later) and reveal characteristic flaws, blemishes, or cracks. In other words, the loupe can provide the necessary information to help you know whether the stone is in fact what it is supposed to be.

For the beginner, the loupe is useful in seeing these features:

1. *The workmanship that went into the cutting.* For example, is the symmetry of the stone balanced? Does it have the proper number of facets for its cut? Is the proportion good? Few cutters put the same time and care into cutting glass as they do into a diamond.

2. *Chips, cracks, or scratches on the facet edges, planes, or table.* White zircon, for example, looks very much like diamond because of its pronounced brilliance and relative hardness, but it chips easily. Therefore, careful examination of a zircon will often show chipping, especially on the top and around the edges. Glass, which is very soft, will often show scratches. Normal wear can cause it to chip or become scratched. Also, if you check around the prongs, the setter may even have scratched it while bending the prongs to hold the stone.

3. *The sharpness of the facet edges.* Harder stones will have a sharp edge, or sharper boundaries between adjoining planes or facets, whereas many imitations are softer, so that under the loupe the edges between the facets are less sharp and have a more rounded appearance.

4. *Bubbles, inclusions, and flaws.* Many flaws and inclusions that cannot be seen with the naked eye can be seen with the loupe. But remember, many are not easily seen unless you are very experienced. With minimal experience, however, the amateur can even learn to spot the characteristic bubbles and swirl lines associated with glass.

When you use a loupe, remember that you won't see what the experienced professional will see—clues about the diamond's quality, authenticity, and durability—but with a little practice, it can still be a valuable tool and might save you from a costly mistake.

CHAPTER THREE

Looking for a Diamond That's a "Cut Above"

One of the most important things to learn is how to look at a diamond, even if you won't see all that a gemologist will. Let's begin by making sure you understand the terms you will be hearing and using to describe what you want—especially terms pertaining to the stone's "cut" and the names for the parts of a cut stone.

It's important to be familiar with a few general terms that are commonly used in reference to faceted stones. The parts of a stone can vary in proportion and thus affect its brilliance, beauty, and desirability. This will be discussed later in greater detail.

- *Girdle.* The girdle is the edge or border of the stone that forms its perimeter; it is the edge formed where the top portion of the stone meets the bottom portion—its "dividing line." This is the part usually grasped by the prongs of a setting.
- *Crown.* The crown is also called the *top* of the stone. This is simply the upper portion of the stone: the part above the girdle.
- *Pavilion.* The pavilion is the bottom portion of the stone, the part from the girdle to the "point" at the bottom.
- *Culet.* The culet is the lowest part or point of the stone. It may be missing in some stones, which can indicate damage.
- *Table.* The table is the flat top of the stone and is the

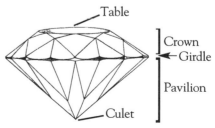

Parts of a faceted stone

stone's largest facet, often called the face. The term *table spread* is used to describe the width of the table facet, often expressed as a percentage of the total width of the stone.

The Cut of the Stone

The most important—and least understood—factor that must be evaluated when one considers any gem is the *cutting*. When we talk about cut, we are not referring to the shape but to the care and precision used in creating a finished gem from the rough. There are many popular shapes for diamonds. Each shape affects the overall look of the stone, but if the stone is cut well its brilliance and value endure no matter what shape it is. For the average consumer, choosing a shape is simply a matter of personal taste. Some of the most popular shapes are pictured. New shapes are discussed in chapter 5.

Classic Shapes

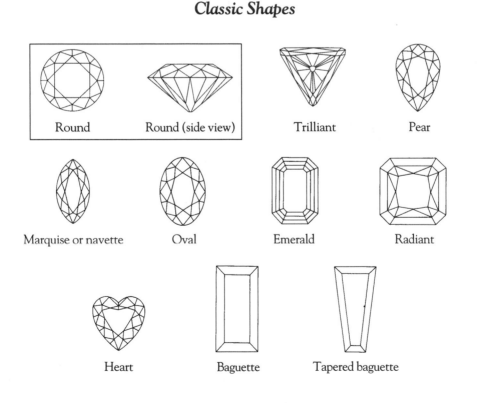

Round   Round (side view)   Trilliant   Pear

Marquise or navette   Oval   Emerald   Radiant

Heart   Baguette   Tapered baguette

Make Makes a Big Difference

The shape of the stone may affect the personality it displays, but it is the overall cutting that releases its full beauty. A term used by professionals to describe the overall quality of the cutting is *make*. Having a "good make" is especially important in diamonds. A diamond with an "excellent make" will sell for much more than one with a "fair make." The difference in price between a well-cut diamond and one that is poorly cut can be as much as 50 percent or more. Even more important, careless cutting, or cutting to get the largest possible stone from the rough, can sometimes result in faults that may make a stone more fragile and vulnerable to breakage. Such stones should sell for much less, although the fault may not be visible without careful examination by an expert. Here we will discuss cutting in a general way. It will be discussed in greater detail later.

How to Know If a Stone Is Well Cut

The precision of the cutting dramatically affects the beauty and value of any stone. This is especially true in *faceted* stones, those on which a series of tiny flat planes (facets or faces) have been cut and polished. By following some general guidelines and tips for looking at faceted gemstones, you can better determine both the quality of the stone and the quality of the cut.

The first thing to keep in mind is that in any stone, if the basic material is of good quality, the way it is cut will make the difference between a dull, lifeless stone and a beautiful, brilliant one. In diamonds, the cutting and proportioning have the greatest influence on the stone's brilliance and fire.

Look at the stone face up, through the top (table). This is the most critical area to view, since this is the one most often noticed. As you look at a diamond, does it seem to sparkle and dance across the whole stone, or are there dead spots?

A quick way to check the symmetry of a round diamond is to look at the table edges. The lines should be straight, regular, and parallel to one another. The table edges should form a regular octagon, with the edges meeting in sharp points. If the lines of the table are wavy, the overall symmetry is not good, and the symmetry of the adjoining facets will also be affected.

  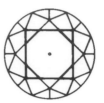

| Table centered but not symmetrical | Table off-center and asymmetrical | Table centered and symmetrical—the ideal |

Next, look at the stone from the side. Note the proportion of the stone both above and below the girdle.

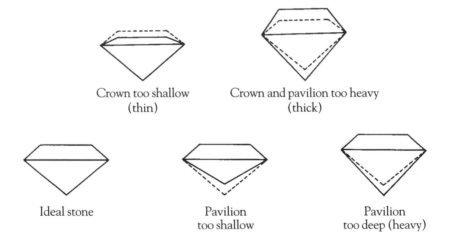

Crown too shallow (thin)   Crown and pavilion too heavy (thick)

Ideal stone   Pavilion too shallow   Pavilion too deep (heavy)

The stone's proportion—whether it is too thin or too thick—will have a marked effect on its overall beauty. The effects of cut and proportioning will be discussed in greater detail in chapter 5, but it is an important first step to become aware of general views and to begin to have a feeling about what looks "right."

Before Beginning

As you shop for any fine gem or piece of jewelry, keep in mind the importance of visiting fine jewelry stores to look at stones and compare them. Many of the factors discussed in the following chapters will become clearer when you have actual stones before you to examine, and you will gain a deeper understanding and appreciation for the gem you are considering. Knowledgeable jewelers will also be happy to take time to help you understand differences in quality and cost.

Also keep in mind the importance of buying only from a well-trained, reputable jeweler. Remember, you are not an expert. The information provided here should help you begin your search more confidently and gain insights that will make the experience more fun, more challenging, and more fulfilling. But perhaps just as important, I hope it will help you make a wiser decision about the jeweler with whom you decide to do business, and about his or her knowledge, professionalism, and integrity. If so, this book will have provided a valuable service and perhaps saved you from a costly mistake.

PART  TWO

Diamonds

CHAPTER FOUR

What Is a Diamond?

Chemically speaking, a diamond is the simplest of all gemstones. It is plain, crystallized carbon—the same substance, chemically, as the soot left on the inside of a glass globe after the burning of a candle; it is the same substance used in "lead" pencils.

The diamond differs from these in its crystal form, which gives it the desirable properties that have made it so highly prized—its hardness, which gives it unsurpassed wearability; its brilliance; and its fire. (But note that while diamond is the hardest natural substance known, it *can* be chipped or broken if hit hard from certain angles, and if the "girdle"—the edge of the diamond that forms the perimeter—has been cut too thin, it can be chipped with even a modest blow.)

The transparent white (or, more correctly, *colorless*) diamond is the most popular variety, but diamond also occurs in colors. When the color is prominent it is called a *fancy* diamond. Diamond is frequently found in nice yellow and brown shades. Colors such as pink, light blue, light green, and lavender occur much more rarely. In diamonds, the colors seen are usually pastel. Deep colors in hues of red, green, and dark blue are extremely rare. Historically, most colored diamonds have sold for more than their colorless counterparts, except for light yellow or brown varieties. Yellow or brown in *very* pale shades may not be fancy diamonds but *off-color* stones that are very common and sell for much less than colorless diamonds or those with a true "fancy" color.

India was one of the earliest known sources of diamond, and the most important, until the eighteenth-century discovery of diamonds in Brazil. In the nineteenth century, a major diamond discovery was made in South Africa, and the twentieth century saw diamond discoveries in other African nations such as Botswana and Angola, and in Russia, Australia, and most recently Canada. Commercial diamond mining is also taking place in the United States.

Many diamonds mined today have no "jewelry" value because they are too tinted and heavily flawed, but they are used for many industrial purposes. Colorless and fancy-color diamonds remain rare, with red diamond being the rarest and most valuable of all gems.

The Four Factors
That Determine Diamond Value

Diamond quality and value are determined by four factors, which are called the "four Cs." They are often listed as follows:

1. Color (body color or *absence* of color)
2. Clarity (degree of flawlessness)
3. Cutting and proportioning (often referred to as the *make*)
4. Carat weight (which affects the size)

In terms of determining beauty, however, we would rank them in a different order:

1. Cutting and proportioning
2. Color
3. Clarity
4. Carat weight

Finding the Right Combination

Keep in mind, however, that the key to being happy with your diamond purchase is understanding how each of these four Cs affects beauty and durability, cost, and the stone *as a whole*. It may sound complicated at first, but when you begin looking at stones you'll see it really isn't. With a little experience, you'll decide which Cs are most important to you, and you'll know what to look for to get the right combination—one that meets your *emotional* and *financial* needs.

Because each factor is a lesson in itself, I have devoted a chapter to each. I will begin with a discussion of diamond cutting and proportioning because it is the least understood and because I think it's the most important factor in terms of the stone's beauty.

CHAPTER FIVE

The Importance of Cut & Proportion

It is important to distinguish exactly what "cut" means in reference to diamonds and other stones. *Cut* does not mean *shape*. Shape pertains to the outline of the diamond's perimeter. The selection of shape is a matter of individual preference. No matter which shape is selected, its *cutting* must be evaluated.

There are several different cutting styles: *brilliant* cut, *step* cut, or *mixed* cut. A brilliant cut uses many facets, usually triangular and kite-shaped, arranged in a particular way to create maximum brilliance. A step cut uses fewer facets, usually trapezoid or rectangular in shape, arranged in a more linear pattern (as you see in the emerald cut). Although usually less brilliant than those cut in a brilliant style, step-cut diamonds can produce a lively, fiery stone with a very elegant and understated personality. You often see step-cut triangle, square, and trapezoid shapes in Art Deco period jewelry (1920s). A mixed-cut style incorporates elements from both the step-cut and brilliant-cut styles.

The term "cut"—also referred to as the stone's *"make"*—is especially important because of its effect on the beauty and personality of the diamond. When we evaluate the cut, we are really judging the stone's proportioning and finish, the two factors that are most directly related to producing the *fire* (the lovely rainbow colors that flash from within) and *brilliance* (the liveliness, the sparkle) that sets diamond apart from all other gems. Regardless of the shape or cutting style, a stone with an excellent make will be exciting, while a stone with a poor make will look lifeless; it will lack the sparkle and personality we identify with diamond. In addition, diamonds are often cut to make them *appear* larger. But a stone that looks much larger than another of the same weight will not be as beautiful as a smaller stone that is properly cut.

Differences in cutting can also affect the *durability* of a diamond. Some cutting faults weaken the stone and make it more susceptible to breaking or chipping.

Fine cutting requires skill and experience, takes more time, and results in greater loss of the "rough" from which the stone is being cut, resulting in a stone that yields less weight when finished. For all these reasons, a well-cut diamond commands a premium and will cost much more than one that is cut poorly.

There are many popular shapes for diamonds. Each shape affects the overall look of the stone, but if the stone is cut well, beauty and value endure no matter which shape you choose. I will begin the discussion of diamond cutting with the round brilliant cut, since this is the most popular shape.

A modern round brilliant-cut diamond has fifty-eight facets. There are thirty-three on the top, twenty-four on the bottom, plus the culet—the "point" at the bottom, which normally is another tiny facet (although many diamonds today are cut without a culet). Round brilliant-cut stones that are small in size are referred to as "full-cut" to distinguish them from "single-cut" stones that have only seventeen facets, or "Swiss-cut" with only thirty-three facets. Older pieces of jewelry such as heirloom diamond bands, or inexpensive pieces containing numerous stones, often contain these cuts instead of full-cut stones. They have less brilliance and liveliness than full-cuts, but with fewer facets they are easier and less expensive to cut. Rings containing single- or Swiss-cut stones should sell for less than rings with full-cut stones.

When a round brilliant-cut diamond is cut well, its shape displays the most liveliness because it enables the most light to be reflected back up through the top. This means that round brilliant-cut diamonds will have greater brilliance, overall, than other shapes, but other shapes can also be very lively. New shapes are also appearing, some of which compare very favorably to round stones for overall brilliance and liveliness.

As a rule of thumb, if the top portion of the stone (the crown) appears to be roughly one-third of the pavilion depth (distance from girdle to culet), the proportioning is probably acceptable.

Crown height		Crown height measures about ⅓ the pavilion depth.
Pavilion depth	⅓	
	⅓	
	⅓	

A well-proportioned stone

Types of Diamond Proportioning

The proportioning—especially the height of the crown in relation to the depth of the pavilion, and the width of the table facet in relation to the width of the stone—is what determines how much brilliance and fire the stone will have. Several formulas for correct proportioning have been developed for round diamonds. Stones that adhere to these very precise formulas are considered to have an "ideal" make and will cost more than other diamonds because of the extra time and skill required to cut them, and because more diamond "rough" is lost in the cutting.

How Cutting Affects Brilliance

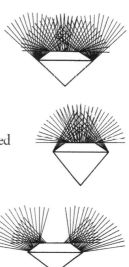

Light Reflection in an Ideally Proportioned Diamond
Ideal proportions ensure the maximum brilliance. When light enters a properly cut diamond, it is reflected from facet to facet, and then back up through the top, exhibiting maximum fire and sparkle.

Light Reflection in a Diamond Cut Too Deep
In a diamond that is cut too deep, much of the light is reflected to opposite facets at the wrong angle and is lost through the sides. The diamond appears dark in the center.

Light Reflection in a Diamond Cut Too Shallow
A diamond cut too shallow (to make it look larger) loses brilliance. The eye sees a ring of dull reflection instead of the great brilliance of a well-cut diamond.

What Is Ideal?

Today great emphasis is placed on "ideal makes" to help people better understand the effect of precision cutting on the beauty and cost of a diamond, and to provide guidelines to help in selecting a diamond that exhibits brilliance, fire, and overall scintillation (the "sparkle" that results from the fire and brilliance working together). There are exceptions to all rules, however, and there are many diamonds that do not adhere to "ideal" parameters, yet are as brilliant and fiery as those that do.

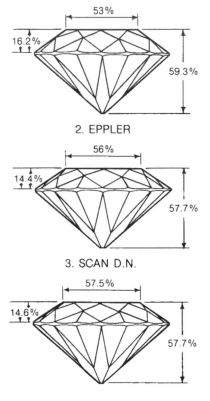

Three standards for "ideal" diamond proportioning

Diamond cutting is an art form that is still evolving, and technological advances continue to shed new insights on how cutting affects the way light travels through diamond to create a scintillating diamond. Today there are several slightly differing formulas for cutting an "ideal" stone, and there is no consensus as to what is "best," but each results in an exceptionally beautiful stone. Generally speaking, diamonds that are cut with smaller tables exhibit more fire; those with larger tables exhibit more brilliance. Larger tables seem to be more in fashion today. But, as common sense may tell you here, both can't excel in the same stone. A larger table can create greater brilliance but may cause some reduction in fire; a smaller table area can increase fire but may reduce brilliance. The ideal would be a compromise that would allow the greatest brilliance and fire simultaneously. No one has come to agreement, however, on what the percentages should be, since some people prefer fire to brilliance, and vice versa. This is one reason why there are several different types of proportioning found in diamonds, and "best" is usually a matter of personal preference.

In 1919, Marcel Tolkowsky developed what he thought would be the best combination of angles to allow light to enter the stone and be reflected back in such a way as to create the most vivid fire combined with intense brilliance. The Tolkowsky cut provided the basis for the modern American ideal make, but today there are several variations of Tolkowsky's formula, some with "brand" names such as the *Lazare Kaplan Ideal*®,

EightStar® Diamond

the *EightStar*®, and the *Hearts on Fire*®. These ideal cuts often create perfectly aligned arrows or a hearts-and-arrows pattern that can be seen with a special viewer. Whatever "ideal" you choose, each results in a very beautiful diamond, but you must compare them for yourself to discover which "ideal" you prefer.

When purchasing a round diamond, ask how the make would be graded: ideal, excellent, very good, good, fair, or poor. A diamond with a "fair" or "poor" make should sell for less than a diamond with a "good" make. A diamond with a "very good," "excellent," or "ideal" make will sell for more. (See chapter 9 for more information on grading the make.)

Keep in mind that despite the effect of cutting on a diamond's beauty, durability, and cost, most laboratories do not yet "grade" the cut or indicate "ideal." The American Gem Society Laboratory (AGS), American Gemological Laboratories (AGL), and Professional Gem Sciences (PGS) do so. Diamond reports from the Gemological Institute of America (GIA) and other laboratories provide information about cutting that relates to the diamond's make, but you must understand how to interpret this information. (See chapter 9.)

Diamonds exhibit somewhat different "personalities" depending on the make. An "ideal" make will exhibit one personality, while another diamond with different proportioning will exhibit a different personality. Not everyone will prefer stones cut to a particular "ideal" formula, and diamonds don't have to be cut to "ideal" proportions to show strong fire and brilliance, to be beautiful or desirable.

I've seen diamonds with "ideal" proportions that were not as brilliant and fiery as diamonds cut to "non-ideal" proportions, and vice versa. Many people prefer diamonds with wider tables than are found in an "ideal," and I have seen diamonds with tables exceeding 64 percent that were surprisingly beautiful and very desirable.

Your eye will be responsible for making the final determination. In general, when you look at a diamond that has a lot of brilliance and fire, the cutting and proportioning probably are acceptable. A stone that appears lifeless and seems to be "dead" or dark at the center probably suffers from poor cutting and proportioning. The more time you take to look at and compare diamonds of different qualities and prices, the better trained your eye will become to detect differences in brilliance and fire, lifelessness and dullness.

No matter what the proportions are, before making a final decision on a particular stone, ask yourself whether or not *you* think it is beautiful. If you like it, don't allow yourself to be overly influenced by formulas.

New Technology Provides *Ideal* Solution

Rather than relying rigidly on formulas or subjective perceptions, new technology may provide the "ideal" solution to the dilemma of judging the overall make of a diamond. Increasingly we are finding new tools on the jewelry store counter—including the *FireScope®*, introduced by EightStar® Diamond Company, the *BrillianceScope™ Analyzer,* and the *BrillianceScope™ Viewer,* developed by GemEx, and the *Gilbertson Scope*—to make it easier for you to know whether or not a diamond is cut to exceptional standards.

One of the first to be developed was the FireScope®. With it, you can compare the cutting of several diamonds side by side very quickly. When a precisely cut diamond—one in which each of the fifty-eight facets has been properly shaped, angled, and aligned—is viewed through the scope, the diamond will produce a pattern showing eight black arrows against a red background. When you see this, you know the diamond exhibits high brilliance, fire, and scintillation.

The BrillianceScope™ Analyzer and the BrillianceScope™ Viewer also enable you to compare several diamonds, but rather than relying on patterns they actually *measure* how much brilliance, fire, and scintillation is seen in the diamond. The latest, the Gilbertson Scope, is similar to the FireScope® but produces a pattern in three colors for a more precise impression of the fire and scintillation.

What is most exciting about these new technologies is that they are providing information about what is really important; that is, what the diamond is *doing* with the light that enters it. With viewers such as those mentioned here, even the most inexperienced consumers will be able to see how light is performing in a specific stone, compare the brilliance and the fire—the overall personality—of different stones, and pick what they really like best. As more jewelers acquire such diamond viewers, it will become much easier for consumers to judge not only the cutting of a diamond, but the final result: its beauty.

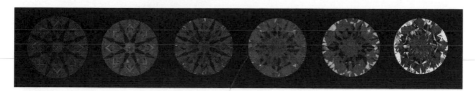

Six diamonds, as seen with the FireScope®, showing the progression of cutting perfection. The diamond on the far right is not very well cut, while the diamond on the far left, one of the "super ideal" cuts known as an EightStar® diamond, shows eight perfect arrows, telling you the diamond is precision-cut; that is, each of the fifty-eight facets is perfectly shaped, angled, and aligned.

Faulty Cuts

Many errors that affect the appearance and value of a diamond can occur in the cutting. Remember that some cutting faults will make a stone more vulnerable to breakage. I recommend avoiding such stones unless they can be protected by the setting.

There are several cutting faults to watch for in round diamonds. First, look carefully for a *sloping table* or a table that is not almost perfectly perpendicular to the point of the culet.

Second, the culet can frequently be the source of a problem. It can be chipped or broken, open or large (almost all modern cut stones have culets that come nearly to a point), off-center, or it can be missing altogether.

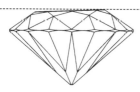

A brilliant-cut stone
with a sloping table

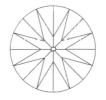

Chipped and "open" culet
(viewed from the bottom)

Off-center culet

Third, repairs to chipped areas can result in *misaligned facets,* which destroy the stone's symmetry.

Sometimes, too, as a result of repair, an *extra facet* will be formed, often in the crown facets, but also on or just below the girdle. These extra facets may slightly affect the stone's brilliance.

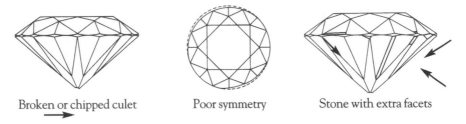

Broken or chipped culet   Poor symmetry   Stone with extra facets

Girdle Faults

The girdle is often the source of faults. *Bearded* or *fringed girdles* are common. A fringed girdle exhibits small radial cracks penetrating into the stone; these can result from a careless or inexperienced cutter. A bearded girdle is similar but not as pronounced a fault and can be easily repaired by repolishing, with minor loss in diamond weight.

The relative thickness of the girdle is very important because it can affect the durability as well as the beauty of the stone. Any girdle can be nicked or chipped in the course of wear, or by careless handling, but if the girdle is too thin it will chip more easily. Some chips can be easily removed by repolishing, with minimal diamond weight loss. If there are numerous chips, the entire girdle can be repolished. Chips or nicks in the girdle are often hidden under the prongs or concealed by the setting.

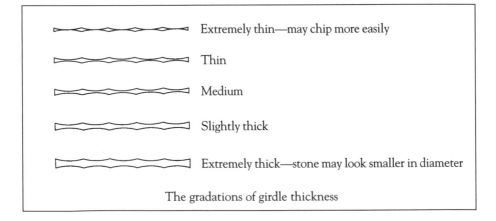

Extremely thin—may chip more easily

Thin

Medium

Slightly thick

Extremely thick—stone may look smaller in diameter

The gradations of girdle thickness

If the girdle is too thick, the stone may look smaller because a disproportionate amount of its weight will be in the girdle itself; such stones, for their weight, will be smaller in diameter than other stones of comparable weight. The girdle can also be *wavy, rough,* or *entirely out-of-round.*

| Wavy girdle | Out-of-round girdle | A natural at the girdle |

A *natural* may not be a fault. It's actually a piece of the natural surface of the diamond crystal. In cutting, a cutter may decide to leave part of the "natural" rough surface in order to get as large a diamond as possible from the rough stone. If this natural is no thicker than the thickness of the girdle and does not distort the circumference of the stone, most dealers consider it a minor defect at worst; if it extends into the crown or pavilion of the stone, it is a more serious fault.

Sometimes if the natural is somewhat large but slightly below the girdle, it will be polished off. This produces an extra facet.

Other Popular Shapes

Unlike round diamonds, "fancy" shapes—all shapes other than round—have no set formulas, so evaluating the make of a fancy is more subjective. Table and depth percentage can vary widely among individual stones of the same shape, each producing a beautiful stone. Personal taste also varies with regard to what constitutes the "ideal" for shapes other than round. Nonetheless, there are certain visual indicators of good or poor proportioning—such as the bow tie effect—which even the amateur can learn to spot. There are recommended ratios for overall shape and symmetry, but a preferred shape is largely a personal matter. Ranges for what is acceptable or unacceptable have been developed (see chapter 9). As you gain experience looking at specific shapes, you will be able to spot faults, and begin to determine what is within an acceptable range. Moderate deviations will not significantly affect the beauty or value of a stone; however, extreme deviations can seriously reduce a stone's beauty and value.

Cutting Faults in Popular Fancy Shapes

One of the most obvious indicators of poor proportioning in fancy shapes is the *bow tie* or *butterfly* effect: a darkened area across the center or widest part of the stone, depending on the cut. The bow tie is most commonly seen in the pear shape or marquise, but it may exist in any fancy shape. Virtually all fancy shapes cut today will exhibit some minimal bow tie effect. Nonetheless, the presence or absence of a bow tie is an indicator of proper proportioning. In poorly proportioned stones there is a pronounced bow tie; the more pronounced, the poorer the proportioning. The less pronounced the bow tie, the better the proportioning. The degree to which the bow tie is evident is the first indicator of a good or a poor make. A diamond with a pronounced bow tie should sell for much less than one without.

Marquise with a pronounced bow tie, or butterfly

As with the brilliant-cut diamond, fancy shapes can also be cut too *broad* or too *narrow,* and the pavilion can be too *deep* or too *shallow.*

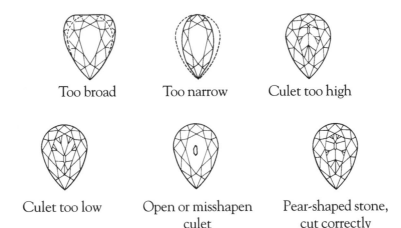

Too broad   Too narrow   Culet too high

Culet too low   Open or misshapen   Pear-shaped stone,
                          culet   cut correctly

Personal taste will always play a role in fancy shapes—some prefer a narrow pear shape, for example, while others might prefer a fatter pear. Whatever the shape you are considering, you must ask yourself whether or not you find the stone exciting. Does it have a pleasing personality?

Does it exhibit good brilliance and fire? Is the entire stone brilliant, or are there "dead" spots? Are there any cutting faults that might make it more susceptible to chipping? Then you must make the choice.

New Shapes Create Excitement

Today we can choose from many shapes and cuts, ranging from the classics—round, oval, pear, marquise, emerald cut, and heart shape—to new shapes that appear as cutters continue to experiment with novel looks. Here are some of the most popular:

The *radiant cut* is perfect for the person who likes the shape of an emerald cut but wants more sparkle. It has the shape of the classic emerald cut—square or rectangular—but much greater brilliance, giving it a per-
Radiant Crisscut®
sonality very similar to a round diamond. The *Crisscut®* is a wonderful blend between the two, more understated than the radiant but livelier than an emerald cut.

The *princess cut,* a square brilliant cut, is ideal for bezel and channel settings (see chapter 13) or any setting in which you want the stone to be flush with the mounting. The *Quadrillion™* was the first
Standard   Quadrillion™
princess
trademarked "princess," cut to unique specifications for maximum brilliance and fire.

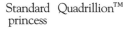

The *trilliant cut,* a popular shape for use as a center stone or as side stones, is also a thin cut, giving a large appearance for its weight. Extra facets
Trilliant Noble Cut™
and precision cutting produce high brilliance. When flanking either side of another diamond, trilliants produce a much larger diamond appearance overall. The *Noble Cut™*, a newly branded elongated "kite" shape with 29 facets, is ideally suited for classic, linear designs.

The *Gabrielle®* cut has 105 facets arranged in a unique alignment that creates more scintillation, more sparkle, than is seen in traditional cuts. The
Gabrielle® comes in all the classic shapes. The *Spirit*
Gabrielle® Spirit Sun®
Sun® is a revolutionary new cut with only 16 facets

and a pointed crown. It represents an entirely new approach to diamond cutting, and its almost pinwheel-like facet alignment achieves intense brilliance and reflectivity.

Tiffany has patented its own new cut, the *Lucida™*, a square brilliant cut that blends the modern brilliant cut and old-mine cut (cushion) with its high crown and small table. This cut is available only

Lucida™   Context®

from Tiffany, although similar cuts are entering the market. Another of the new "square" cuts, the *Context®*, creates a wholly new look. The epitome of simplicity, it can be fashioned only from rare, perfectly formed diamond crystals—one in one hundred thousand—and it achieves an amazing luminosity without altering the inherent shape of the natural crystal.

The *Royal Asscher®* is a contemporary 74-facet version of the original Asscher, an older cut that is enjoying renewed popularity (see page 36). A square cut characterized by exaggerated corners, the Royal Asscher® reveals intense fire.

Royal Asscher®   Modern
cushion

The overall look is elegant, classic, and important. The distinctive *modern cushion cut*, a blend between a rectangular and oval shape, is a contemporary version of a cut that dates back prior to the turn of the nineteenth century (see page 36). The modern version is more brilliant and not as "heavy" in its make, so it looks somewhat larger than earlier cushion cuts of the same weight.

As we learn more and more about diamond cutting and how various facet arrangements and angles affect the way light performs in a diamond, new cuts continue to emerge. These include the *New Century®*, a patented 102-facet, round, super brilliant cut; the Zoë, a scintillating 100-facet cut; the extra fiery 82-facet *Royal 82;* the 80-facet *Spirit of Flanders™;* the *Lily Cut®,* shaped like a four-leaf-clover; the 66-facet *Leo Diamond™;* and the new 97-facet, 12-sided *Escada®* that was created exclusively for the great fashion house.

In addition to the new cuts above, we are also seeing cutting innovations in baguettes, with new brilliant-cut baguettes, such as the *Princette™* and the *Bagillion™*. They occur in straight and tapered shapes. There are also Crisscut® baguettes and tapered baguettes. These are gaining in popularity because they have greater brilliance than traditional baguettes. They can be used to flank diamonds or other stones in traditional settings, or are used in very contemporary jewelry design with straight, clean lines.

Early Cuts Enjoy Renewed Popularity

Interest in antique and period jewelry is growing rapidly. As it does, the diamonds that adorn them are arousing renewed attention and gaining new respect. The way a diamond is cut is often one of the clues to the age of a piece. Older diamonds can be replaced or recut to modern proportions, but replacing or recutting stones mounted in antique or period pieces could adversely affect the value of the jewelry. To preserve the integrity of the piece, antique and period jewelry connoisseurs want original stones, or, if stones have been replaced, at least stones cut in the manner typical of the period. The market is becoming increasingly strong for diamonds with older cuts, and prices are also strengthening.

As these early cut diamonds receive more and more attention, a growing number of people are beginning to appreciate them for their distinctive beauty and personality and for the romance that accompanies them. The romantic element—combined with a cost that is more attractive than that of new diamonds—is also making them an increasingly popular choice for engagement rings.

Some of the earlier cuts are the *table cut,* the *rose cut,* the *old-mine cut,* and the *old-European cut.* (Before 1919, when America began to emerge as an important diamond cutting center, most diamonds were cut in Europe. Thus most "old European" diamonds were cut before the first quarter of the twentieth century.)

The *table cut* illustrates history's earliest cutting effort. By placing the point of a diamond crystal against a turning wheel that held another diamond, the point could be worn down, creating a squarish, flat surface that resembled a *tabletop.* Today we still call the flat facet on the very top of the stone the *table* facet.

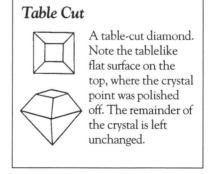

Table Cut

A table-cut diamond. Note the tablelike flat surface on the top, where the crystal point was polished off. The remainder of the crystal is left unchanged.

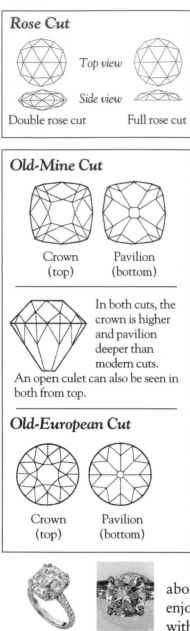

Rose Cut

Top view

Side view

Double rose cut   Full rose cut

Old-Mine Cut

Crown   Pavilion
(top)   (bottom)

In both cuts, the crown is higher and pavilion deeper than modern cuts. An open culet can also be seen in both from top.

Old-European Cut

Crown   Pavilion
(top)   (bottom)

Old Asscher in a   Old
modern setting   cushion cut

The *rose cut* is a sixteenth-century cut, usually with a flat base and facets radiating from the center in multiples of six, creating the appearance of an opening rosebud. The rose cut appears in round, pear, and oval shapes.

The *old-mine* is a precursor to the modern round. This cut has a squarish or "cushion" shape (a rounded square). Proportions follow the diamond crystal, so the crown is higher and the pavilion is deeper than in modern stones. The table is very small, and the culet is very large and is easily seen from the top (resembling a "hole" in the diamond). These lack the brilliance of modern stones but often exhibit tremendous fire. The old-mine is enjoying a resurgence in popularity today.

Appearing in the mid-1800s, the *old-European* is similar to the old-mine cut but is *round* rather than squarish, with fifty-eight facets. The crown is higher than in modern cuts but not as high as in the old-mine cut; it has a deep pavilion, but not as deep as in old-mines. The culet is still "open" but smaller than in old-mines.

In addition to the early cuts described above, there are two other older cuts that are enjoying renewed popularity: the *cushion cut,* with a small table, high crown, and large culet, which resembles the old-mine but is usually more elongated; and the *Asscher cut,* a more or less square emerald cut that, like old-European and old-mine cut diamonds, is characterized by a very high crown, deep pavilion, small table, large culet, and very canted corners (in some cases the angles formed at the corners are so pronounced that the stone resembles an octagon). Although exhibiting less brilliance than modern-cut diamonds, the cushion and Asscher both exhibit very fiery personalities, and offer a distinctive look with a classic character.

Older cutting styles once popular for use as side stones, or to create interesting design elements, are also enjoying renewed popularity. Among the most popular are two *step-cut* shapes—the trapezoid and the half-moon—and the briolette.

Trapezoid Half-moon

The *trapezoid* and *half-moon* are often seen in Art Deco period jewelry (1910 into the 1920s) and make especially elegant choices to use with emerald-cut diamonds (which are also step cut) and colored gemstones. Here the understated character of the trapezoid or half-moon is very complementary; while lively, their brilliance is not overpowering as it often is with modern brilliant cuts.

Briolette

The *briolette* is fashioned into a "drop," completely encircled with tiny triangular facets. A single briolette can be worn as a pendant, or multiple briolettes can be suspended from almost any piece of jewelry. We are again seeing briolettes used in earrings and brooches and suspended in multiples, like a fringe, from necklaces.

Are Diamonds with Old Cuts Valuable?

Old cuts can be very beautiful. The finest examples of these earlier cutting styles exhibit intense fire and have tremendous allure, especially among collectors and those who appreciate authentic jewelry from these earlier periods. By today's standards, however, they lack brilliance, and a very large culet may detract from the stone's beauty.

Until recently, old-mine cut and old-European cut diamonds have been evaluated by comparison with modern-cut stones. Value has been determined by estimating the color, the clarity, and the weight the stone would *retain* if it were recut to modern proportions. However, this practice is now changing because of the increasing demand for old cuts, as mentioned earlier.

I don't suggest recutting old diamonds if they are in their original mountings. The overall integrity of the piece—and its value—would be adversely affected.

If the setting has no special merit, the decision must be an individual one, based on whether or not the stone appeals to you. As I have said, some older cuts are very lovely, while others may look heavy, dull, or lifeless. An unattractive older cut may benefit from recutting, and although it will lose weight, it may have equal or greater value because of the improved make. In addition, recutting can sometimes improve the clarity grade of an older stone. Finally, before deciding whether or not to recut, you should note that the increasing popularity of older cuts is driving prices higher since they are difficult to find. In addition to their unique personalities, old cuts can have a distinctive character that sets them apart from more modern cuts.

Retail Price Guide for Old-European Cut Diamonds*

Prices are per carat in U.S. dollars

Color	½ Carat	1 Carat	2–3 Carat
Color D–F			
VVS–VS	6,500–7,500	9,200–13,000	14,600–26,000
SI	4,875	7,000–9,600	12,400–13,200
I_1	3,250	5,000	5,600–7,000
Color G–H			
VVS–VS	5,500–6,450	7,200–10,000	11,200–14,000
SI	4,625	6,400–8,800	10,000–11,000
I_1	2,875	5,500–6,000	6,300–7,500
Color I			
VVS–VS	4,375	6,800	9,000–11,000
SI	3,690	6,000	8,000–8,800
I_1	2,375	5,000	7,000–7,250
Color J–K			
VVS–VS	3,975	6,200–7,250	8,000–9,600
SI	3,250	6,250	6,400–7,200
I_1	2,125	4,625	6,000–7,000
Color L–M			
VVS–VS	3,250	6,250	6,400–7,200
SI	2,500	5,500	6,250–7,000
I_1	1,875	4,000	4,500–5,500

*Retail prices are based on information provided by Michael Goldstein Ltd.

Retail Price Guide for Rose-Cut Diamonds*

Prices are per carat in U.S. dollars

Size	Carat	Color	Per Carat
3–4 mm	0.15–0.20	H–J,VS–SI	1,375–1,625
		K–M,VS–SI	1,200–1,500
5 mm	0.45	H–J,VS–SI	2,000–2,500
		K–M,VS–SI	1,750–2,250
6 mm	0.75	H–J,VS–SI	2,500–3,375
		K–M,VS–SI	1,750–2,000

*Retail prices are based on information provided by Michael Goldstein Ltd.

Retail Price Guide for Briolette-Cut Diamonds*

Prices are for bright goods, VS to SI clarity, and are per carat in U.S. dollars

Weight	Brown	Cognac	K–M	H–I
½ carat	375–600	750–1,050	1,375–1,750	2,440–2,750
¾ carat	600–750	1,050–1,350	1,875–2,250	3,000–3,500
1 carat	1,050	1,250–1,500	2,440–3,000	3,750–4,500

*Retail prices are based on information provided by Michael Goldstein Ltd.

A Word about Recutting Diamonds

There are many fine diamond cutters in the United States—New York City is one of the most important diamond cutting centers in the world for top-quality diamonds—and many diamonds can be greatly improved by recutting.

If you have an old-cut diamond that you don't care for, or a damaged diamond, your jeweler can consult with a diamond cutter—or refer you to one—to determine whether or not your stone can be improved by recutting and, if so, what risks and costs might be involved.

Normally, the cost to recut a diamond ranges from approximately $150 *per carat* to as much as $350 *per carat,* depending on the skill required and the labor involved. In rare instances, the cost might be more. Thus, if the labor estimate to recut a stone is $150 per carat, recutting a two-carat diamond will cost $300.

A knowledgeable jeweler can help you decide whether or not a diamond should be recut, make arrangements for you, and help assure you that you've received the same stone back. For your own comfort and security, as well as the cutter's, I recommend that you obtain a diamond grading report or a thorough appraisal before having a stone recut, so that you have a point of reference when the stone is returned.

To What Extent Does Cutting & Proportioning Affect Value in Modern Diamonds?

Excellently cut and proportioned stones cost significantly more per carat than those that are not cut well. The following will give a very basic idea of how some of the most frequently encountered defects can affect a diamond's price.

- Table is not a reasonably accurate octagon—2 to 15 percent off
- Girdle is too thick—5 to 10 percent off
- Girdle is too thin—5 to 25 percent off
- Symmetry of crown facets off—5 to 15 percent on round, less on fancy cuts since defect is not so easily seen
- Asymmetrical culet—2 to 5 percent off
- Misaligned culet—5 to 25 percent off
- Stone too shallow—15 to 50 percent off
- Stone too thick—10 to 30 percent off
- Thin crown—5 to 20 percent off
- Thick crown—5 to 15 percent off

As you can see, there is a fairly wide range here, depending upon the severity of the error, and only an experienced professional can determine the extent to which the value of a given stone may be lessened. But a quick computation shows that a stone suffering from several errors (which is fairly common) could certainly have a significantly reduced price per carat.

Remember: The value of two diamonds with the same weight, color, and clarity can differ dramatically because of differences in cutting.

CHAPTER SIX

Body Color

Color is one of the most important factors to consider when select-ing a diamond because one of the first things most people notice is whether or not the diamond is white, or, more accurately, *colorless* (there actually are *white* diamonds, usually milky white in color and translucent, but they are very rare and most people do not find them attractive). The color grade of a diamond, a measure of the stone's *col-orlessness*, is also one of the most significant factors affecting value.

Color refers to the natural body color of a diamond. The finest and most expensive "white" diamonds are absolutely colorless, as in pure springwater. Most diamonds show some trace of yellowish or brownish tint. Diamonds also occur in every color of the rainbow. Natural-colored diamonds are called *fancy-color* diamonds.

How to Look at a Diamond to Evaluate Color

In colorless diamonds, color differences from one grade to the next can be very subtle, and a difference of several grades is difficult to see when a diamond is mounted. Keep in mind that it is impossible to accu-rately grade color in a mounted diamond. When looking at an unmount-ed stone, however, even an amateur can learn to see color differences if the stone is viewed properly.

Because of the diamond's high brilliance and dispersion (fire), the color grade cannot be accurately determined by looking at the stone from the top, or face-up, position. It is best to observe color by examining the stone through the *pavilion,* with the table down. Use a flat white surface such as a folded white business card, or a grading trough, which can be purchased from a jewelry supplier.

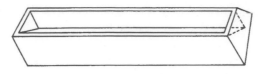

A grading trough, available in plastic or in
handy disposable folding white cardboard
stand-up packs. Be sure to use a *clean* trough.

Position 1. Place table-side down and view the stone
through the pavilion facets.

Position 2. Table-side down, view the stone through the
plane of the girdle.

Position 3. Place the pavilion down with the culet pointing
toward you. View the stone through the girdle
plane.

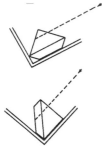

Position 4. Place table-down in a grading trough and view
the stone through the girdle plane.

Position 5. Place pavilion-down in a grading trough, with
the culet pointing toward you. View the stone
through the pavilion facets.

What Is Body Color?

When we discuss body color in colorless diamonds, we mean how
much yellow or brown tint can be seen. We are not referring to rare natural-color diamonds.

Today, most colorless diamonds in the United States and other countries are graded on an alphabetical scale beginning with the letter D.
This letter designation is part of a color grading system introduced by

the Gemological Institute of America (GIA) and is used extensively in the diamond trade worldwide. The GIA classification progresses from D, the rarest classification on this scale (colorless), through the alphabet to Z, getting progressively more tinted. The grades D, E, and F are exceptionally rare and are the only grades that should be referred to as colorless. (Technically, E and F are not colorless, since they possess a trace of yellow or brown, but the tint is so slight that referring to them as colorless is acceptable.)

A diamond with the color grade D exhibits the most prized color. It is essentially colorless—like crystal-clear springwater—and is considered the most desirable. Diamonds with D-color are very rare, and a significant premium is paid for them. A diamond with the color grade E also is exceptionally rare and is almost indistinguishable from D except to the very experienced. Nonetheless, diamonds graded E in color cost significantly less per carat than those graded D, despite the difficulty in seeing the difference. The next color grade is F, and it is close to E, but there is more gradation in color than the difference observed between D and E.

What Color Grade Is Most Desirable?

The colors D, E, and F can all be grouped as exceptionally fine, rare colors and may be referred to as *colorless, exceptional white,* or *rare white,* as they are often described by diamond dealers. The colors G and H may be referred to as *fine white* or *rare white.* These grades are also rare and considered very fine. The I and J colors are slightly more tinted than G and H, and sell for less, but diamonds possessing color grades G through J are very fine colors and are classified as *near colorless.* The colors K and L show a stronger tint of yellow or brown, but settings can often mask the tint. Grades M through Z will show progressively more and more tint of yellowish or brownish color. Grades D through J seem to have better resale potential than grades K through Z. This does not mean, however, that diamonds having less rare color grades are less beautiful or desirable. Sometimes a more tinted diamond can exhibit a warmth not shown by other diamonds and create a very beautiful ring with a unique appeal.

To What Extent Does the Color Grade Affect Value?

To an untrained eye, discerning the difference in color from D down to H in a mounted stone, without direct comparison, is almost impossible. Nevertheless, the difference in color greatly affects the value of the diamond. A one-carat, flawless, excellently proportioned, D-color diamond might retail for $30,000, while the same stone with H-color might sell for only $12,000 and the same stone with K-color might sell for only $7,500. And, of course, if the stone were not flawless, it could sell for much less (see next chapter). This sounds complicated, but color differences and their effect on price will become clear to you the moment you begin looking at stones. It is important to understand your options and to be watchful when you go to purchase a stone.

Diamond Color Grades

COLORLESS	D E F	Loose diamonds appear colorless.
NEAR COLORLESS	G H I J	When mounted in a setting, these diamonds may appear colorless to the untrained eye.
FAINT YELLOWISH* TINT	K L M	Smaller diamonds look colorless when mounted. Diamonds of ½ carat or more show traces of color.
VERY LIGHT YELLOWISH* TINT	N O P Q R	These diamonds show increasingly yellow tints to even the untrained eye, and appear very "off-white."
TINTED LIGHT YELLOWISH*	S T U V W X Y Z	

* Usually yellow, but can be brown or gray

Commonly Used Diamond Color Grading Systems

The GIA and American Gem Society (AGS) grading systems are the most commonly used in the United States. The GIA system is the most widely used in the world. Scandinavian diamond nomenclature (Scan D.N.) is often used in Scandinavian countries, as well as a system developed by CIBJO (the International Confederation of Jewelry, Silverware, Diamonds, Pearls, and Stones). Participating member nations include most European nations, Japan, and the United States. Another system, HRD, is applied by the Belgian Diamond High Council.

Appearance	AGS	GIA	SCAN D.N. UNDER 0.50 CARAT	SCAN D.N. 0.50 CARAT AND OVER	CIBJO UNDER 0.47 CARAT	CIBJO 0.47 CARAT AND OVER	HRD
Mounted stones appear colorless	0	D	White	River	Exceptional white	Exceptional white (†)	Exceptional white (†)
	0	E	White	River	Exceptional white	Exceptional white	Exceptional white
	1	F	White	Top wesselton	Rare white	Rare white (†)	Rare white (†)
	2	G	White	Top wesselton	Rare white	Rare white	Rare white
	3	H	White	Wesselton	White	White	White
	4	I	Slightly tinted white	Top crystal	Slightly tinted white	Slightly tinted white (I)	Slightly tinted white
Mounted stones appear increasingly tinted	5	J	Slightly tinted white	Crystal	Slightly tinted white	Slightly tinted white (J)	Slightly tinted white
	6	K	Tinted color	Top cape	Tinted white	Tinted white (K)	Tinted white
	6	L	Tinted color	Top cape	Tinted white	Tinted white (L)	Tinted white
	7	M	Tinted color	Cape	Tinted color	Tinted color	Tinted color
	7	N	Tinted color	Cape	Tinted color	Tinted color	Tinted color
	8	O	Tinted color	Cape	Tinted color	Tinted color	Tinted color
	8	P	Tinted color	Light yellow	Tinted color	Tinted color	Tinted color
	8	Q	Tinted color	Light yellow	Tinted color	Tinted color	Tinted color
Mounted stones appear yellow	9-10*	R	Tinted color	Light yellow	Tinted color	Tinted color	Tinted color
	9-10*	S-X -Z	Tinted color	Yellow	Tinted color	Tinted color	Tinted color

Side brackets: "Small mounted stones appear colorless" (spanning AGS 0–5); "Mounted stones appear colorless" (AGS 0–4).

*AGS grade 9 corresponds to GIA, R–U inclusive. AGS grade 10 corresponds to GIA, V–Z inclusive.

† The use of the term *blue-white* is discouraged today, since it is usually misleading.

In diamonds over one carat, the whiter the stone, the more critical it becomes to know the exact color grade because of its effect on value. On the other hand, as long as you know for sure what color the stone is and are paying the right price, choosing one that is a grade or two lower than another will reduce the cost per carat but there will be little, if any, visible difference when the stone is mounted. Therefore, for the difference in cost, you might be able to get a larger diamond, or one with better cutting or a better clarity grade, depending on what is most important to you.

Natural Color or HPHT Processed

Color differences can be subtle, but the difference in cost can be extreme. It is important to know the precise color grade, but it is even more important to know whether the color is natural or the result of some type of treatment. In chapter 10, I discuss several fraudulent techniques that have been used for many years to "whiten" tinted diamonds. Until recently, these treatments produced results that were only temporary, and any competent gemologist could detect the treatment. This has changed rapidly in the past few years, however, and new techniques are creating permanent results. Perhaps more important, detection often requires very sophisticated testing. On the one hand, what has been developed is very exciting, but on the other hand it provides yet another reason to take precautions to ensure you are buying what you think you are buying.

A new product entered the market in the 1990s, resulting from years of research conducted in a joint-venture between a diamond manufacturer and General Electric. Briefly, the product was created by a new process involving the use of high-pressure/high-temperature annealing (often referred to as the *HPHT* process). With it, very tinted, off-white diamonds can be transformed into colorless and near-colorless stones, ranging from D through H in color. In addition to using this process to create colorless through near-colorless stones, the process can also be used to produce "fancy" colors, including yellow, yellowish green, pink, and blue (see page 97).The innovators of this process believe they have created a new diamond category that will provide new alternatives to consumers. The color of these stones, originally referred to as *GE-POL* diamonds, is permanent and irreversible.

Not all tinted diamonds can be transformed into colorless or near-colorless diamonds. Only very rare diamond types respond to HPHT whitening techniques. Of all the diamonds mined, reports estimate that fewer than 2 percent produce the desired effect. Today the process is also being used to produce fancy-color yellow, pink, and blue diamonds.

The color-enhanced "colorless" diamonds produced by GE are now sold under the name Bellataire™ through exclusive arrangements with selected retailers. They are usually cut in fancy shapes (approximately 85 percent) and are available in color grades from D through H, with clarity grades VS$_2$ or better (see chapter 7 for a discussion on clarity grades). In an effort to communicate clearly and honestly, each diamond is laser inscribed on the girdle with the Bellataire logo and a registered number, but there have been cases where the laser inscription has been polished off.

In terms of cost, it is unclear how they will be priced. Some retailers are charging a small premium because of the rarity of these diamonds, while others are providing an incentive to customers by pricing them at 15 to 20 percent below their natural-color counterparts. For many, these newcomers are a beautiful and exciting "high-tech" alternative. Ultimately, however, it will be consumer acceptance and demand that will determine their pricing.

In addition to Bellataire™ colorless and fancy yellow, blue, and pink diamonds, other companies are using HPHT annealing techniques to whiten diamonds and to produce a range of colors. Lucent Diamonds™ *Luminari* brand offers a wide range of yellow, deep yellow, orange-yellow, and yellow-green diamonds, and Nova™ Diamonds is offering yellowish green to greenish yellow, among other colors. Diamonds are even being transformed into mysterious *black* diamonds through HPHT methods, and who knows what alluring colors await us in the future. In fancy colors, these treated diamonds should sell for significantly less than natural-color fancy diamonds.

Many people are intrigued by these stones, and find them a very attractive alternative to other diamonds. Labs such as the GIA, the Swiss Gemmological Institute (SSEF), and the European Gemological Laboratory (EGL) will grade diamonds treated in this manner, indicating the use of this process on the report, usually under "Comments" (see chapter 9). GIA also requires that the words "HPHT Processed" be laser-inscribed on the stone's girdle before issuing the grading report. However, caution needs to be taken. Once again, the availability of this new product in the marketplace provides yet another reason to obtain laboratory verification prior to the purchase of any important diamond. There have already been incidents of HPHT-treated diamonds having been sold without disclosure of the treatment. More importantly, before becoming aware of the use of this technology on diamonds, gem-testing laboratories were not checking for it, nor did they have the data to understand how to detect it. Today most diamonds treated in this manner can be identified, but prior to the year 2000, HPHT-treated stones may have slipped through the world's labs undetected. See chapter 10 for more advice on how to protect yourself from buying an HPHT diamond unknowingly.

What Is Fluorescence?

If the diamond you are considering is accompanied by a diamond grading report issued by the GIA or another respected lab, it will indicate whether or not the diamond has some degree of *fluorescence*. Fluorescence refers to whether or not a stone produces a color reaction when exposed to ultraviolet radiation—a color seen *only* when the stone is exposed to ultraviolet radiation. Whether or not a diamond fluoresces, and the strength of its fluorescence (faint, weak, moderate, strong, very strong) are determined by viewing the diamond with a special lamp called an ultraviolet lamp, which emits only ultraviolet radiation. When we say a colorless diamond fluoresces blue, we mean that its color will appear to be blue when we view it under the pure ultraviolet light produced by the ultraviolet lamp. The stone is really a colorless diamond and will appear colorless in normal light. Some diamonds fluoresce; others do not. A diamond can fluoresce any color, but most diamonds fluoresce blue, white, or yellow.

It is important to note whether or not a diamond fluoresces, and what color it fluoresces, because there are varying wavelengths of ultraviolet radiation all around us. Ultraviolet radiation is present in daylight (that's what causes sunburn) and wherever there are fluorescent light fixtures (those long tube lights you see in the ceilings of many stores and office buildings). This means that, depending upon the strength of a diamond's fluorescence and the intensity of the ultraviolet radiation in the light source, its color may not appear the same in all lights.

A diamond that fluoresces a strong blue, for example, might appear whiter in daylight, or in an office with fluorescent lights, because the ultraviolet radiation present will cause the diamond to emit some degree of blue, masking any faint yellow or brown tint that might be present. The same stone might appear less white when seen at home in incandescent light—any warm light, such as a household lightbulb—where you see the stone's true body color without the benefit of any fluorescence stimulated by ultraviolet radiation. A diamond that fluoresces "strong yellow" can look more yellow in some lights. But remember, whatever color is produced by fluorescence, it occurs *only* in daylight or fluorescent light.

To ensure that the true body color is being graded, a professional always tests a diamond for fluorescence with an ultraviolet lamp before color grading it. Blue fluorescence is more common than white or yellow. Some diamonds that fluoresce blue may actually look blue-white in the right light.

The results of a recent study conducted by the GIA showed that consumers found the presence of blue fluorescence to be a benefit; participants in the study actually preferred diamonds that fluoresced blue to other diamonds because they seemed "whiter," despite the fact that you will not really notice fluorescence with the naked eye.

Does Fluorescence Affect Value?

Generally, the presence or absence of fluorescence has little if any effect on value. However, if the stone has a strong yellow fluorescence it may sell for 10 to 15 percent less, since this will make the stone appear more yellow in some lights than another stone with the same color grade.

Blue fluorescence may be considered an added benefit—a little bonus—because it may make the stone appear whiter in some lights, and yet there may be no difference in cost or the stone may sell at a modest *discount* (although this may change after the results of the GIA study). You must be careful, however, to look closely at stones with *very strong* blue fluorescence—some will have an oily or murky appearance. If the stone appears murky or oily in daylight or fluorescent light, it should sell for 15 to 20 percent less than comparable stones without the murky cast.

If a diamond fluoresces, its true body color can be misgraded. This can be costly to the buyer, but the error can be easily avoided. Knowledgeable jewelers or appraisers will always test a diamond to see whether or not it fluoresces, and to what degree, in order to color grade it accurately.

What Is a "Premier"?

At this point I should mention a type of fluorescent diamond that is not encountered often, but which occurs frequently enough to warrant a brief discussion. It is called a *premier*. This does not mean the diamond is better than others. In fact, it should sell for much less than other white diamonds.

The true color of any premier diamond will be yellowish (referred to in the trade as *cape*), but the yellow color is masked by strong blue fluorescence. As with other diamonds that fluoresce blue, the premier will appear whiter than it really is in certain light. It may actually have a bluish tint, sometimes with a greenish cast. However, a premier will *always* have a murky or oily appearance in daylight or fluorescent light, resulting from the coupling of the yellow with the blue. The murkiness detracts from its beauty and causes a reduction in value. The price of the premier varies depending on the degree of yellow present and the degree of murkiness.

Do not confuse a premier diamond with one that exhibits normal blue fluorescence. Many diamonds exhibit some degree of fluorescence. Many have a very fine white body color to begin with. But most important, they differ from the premier because they will not appear oily or murky in daylight-type light.

What Is a Chameleon Diamond?

A chameleon diamond is one that changes color when heated or exposed to light. But the color is not permanent and will revert back to its original color. Several diamonds that show this very unusual phenomenon have been sold recently at auction for impressive prices, and they make interesting conversation pieces. Whatever color they exhibit in natural or fluorescent light, or when heated, usually becomes more yellow when they are left in the dark for a time.

Special Tips on the Subject of Color

Keep It Clean if You Want the Color to Look Its Best

A dirty diamond will not look white, nor will it sparkle. An accumulation of dirt, especially greasy dirt, will give a diamond a yellowish cast, so if you want to see and enjoy its full beauty, keep your diamond clean.

This principle applies especially when you are looking at old jewelry for possible purchase. When you are considering old diamond pieces, pay particular attention to whether or not it is impacted with dirt accumulated by years of use. If it is, there is a possibility that the diamond will have a better color grade than it may appear to have at first glance. This is because the dirt may contain varying amounts of fatty deposits (from dishwashing, cosmetics, etc.), which yellow with age. When this type of dirt builds up and is in contact with the diamond, it will also make the diamond appear more yellow.

White or Yellow Gold Setting?

The color of the metal in the setting can affect your perception of the color of the stone—sometimes adversely and sometimes beneficially. A very white diamond should be held in a white metal such as white gold, platinum, or palladium. If you prefer yellow gold, it's possible to have just the portion of the setting that holds the diamond itself fashioned in white metal. For example, a diamond ring can be made with a yellow gold shank to go around the finger and a white metal head to hold the diamond. An all-yellow setting may make a very white diamond appear less white because the yellow color of the setting itself is reflected into the diamond.

On the other hand, if the diamond you choose tends to be more yellow than you'd like, mounting it in yellow gold, with yellow surrounding the stone, may make the stone appear whiter in contrast to the strong yellow of the gold.

The yellow gold environment may mask the degree of yellow in a yellow diamond, or it may give a colorless diamond an undesirable yellow tint. The setting can also affect future color grading should you ever need an updated insurance appraisal. (For information on gold and platinum, see *Jewelry & Gems—The Buying Guide: How to Buy Diamonds, Pearls, Colored Gemstones, Gold & Jewelry with Confidence and Knowledge.*)

CHAPTER SEVEN

Clarifying Clarity:
How Flaws Affect Diamonds

Flaw classification—also called *clarity* grade—is one of the criteria used to determine the value of a diamond. As with all things in nature, however, there is really no such thing as "flawless." Even though some very rare diamonds are classified "flawless," the term is somewhat misleading, and you must be sure you understand what it really means.

When we talk about this classification, we are referring to the presence of tiny, usually microscopic, characteristics. The word *flaw* suggests something bad, but this is not really the case; rather, the flaw grade simply provides part of the complete description of the stone. It is important to understand that as diamonds form in nature, *every* diamond develops certain types of internal characteristics. They might be microscopic cracks shaped like feathers—some are quite lovely when viewed with the microscope—or microscopic diamond crystals, or even crystals of some other gemstone!

Every diamond contains distinctive internal characteristics. In the jewelry trade, these internal characteristics are called *inclusions,* something *included* within the stone as it was forming in nature. Each diamond's internal picture—its internal character—is unique. No two are alike, so the clarity picture can be an important factor in identifying a specific diamond.

To What Extent Does Clarity Affect the Beauty of a Diamond?

It is very important to understand that clarity may have little or no effect on the beauty of a diamond if it falls within the first eight clarity grades discussed later in this chapter (FL through SI). Few people can discern any visible difference between stones until they reach the imperfect grades, and even then it is sometimes difficult to see anything in the stone without magnification.

Many people mistakenly believe that the clarity grade affects a diamond's brilliance and sparkle. This is not true; the clarity grade has little effect on a diamond's visible appearance except in the very lowest grades. Many people think that the better the clarity, the more brilliant and sparkling the diamond. Perhaps it is the term itself, *clarity,* that leads to the confusion (and the reason I don't like the term *clarity grade*). Whatever the case, as discussed in chapter 5, it is the precision of the *cutting* that determines how brilliant and sparkling a diamond will be.

To the buyer, the flaw grade, or clarity grade, is important because it indicates, on a relative basis, how "clean" the diamond is, and this ranking has a significant effect on cost. The cleaner the stone, the rarer; the rarer the stone, the costlier. But diamonds don't have to be flawless to be beautiful and sparkling.

As you will see when you shop and compare, you can find very beautiful, sparkling diamonds in a wide range of clarity grades. Juggling the clarity grade can give you tremendous flexibility in getting a whiter or larger diamond for your money. Just keep in mind that you won't see differences with the eye alone, so you must take care to know for sure what the specific clarity grade is.

How Is the Clarity Grade Determined?

Diamonds used in jewelry are usually very clean, and little if anything can be seen without magnification. This is starting to change as an increasing number of diamonds with visible cracks or other inclusions enter the market—stones in the I_1 through I_3 range and below—but for the most part, differences in clarity cannot normally be seen simply by looking at the stone with the naked eye. The clarity grade is based on what can be seen *when the diamond is examined with 10x magnification* under a loupe (see chapter 2). The clarity grade is based on the number, size, color, and location of inclusions or blemishes in the stone. The flawless grade is given to a stone in which no imperfections can be seen internally (inclusions) or externally (blemishes) when examined with

10x magnification, although at higher powers inclusions will be visible even in a flawless diamond. For clarity grading purposes, if an inclusion can't be seen at 10x, it doesn't exist.

Clarity grading requires extensive training and practice, and proper grading can be done only by an experienced jeweler, dealer, or gemologist. If you want to examine a diamond with the loupe, remember that only in the lowest grades will an inexperienced person be able to see inclusions or blemishes easily, and even with the loupe it will be difficult to see what a professional will see easily. Few amateurs will see anything at all in the highest clarity grades.

Today, a jeweler might use a microscope with a video monitor to help you see what is inside a diamond you are considering. Be sure that the jeweler focuses at different depths into the stone and that the microscope is set at 10x (higher power may actually conceal something in the diamond because of the difficulty in focusing properly at higher powers). And remember: don't panic—what you are seeing is magnified ten times!

I recommend that you first examine the stone carefully with your eyes alone, then with a simple loupe, saving the microscope, when offered, for last. Examining a diamond in this way will help you become familiar with the particular characteristics of the stone you purchase, and may give you information that will enable you to always recognize your diamond should it be necessary at some future time (after having it mounted in the ring, for example).

Types of Internal and External Characteristics

Basically, clarity grading systems grade the stone according to the presence or absence of internal and external characteristics, generally referred to as "flaws." They are called *inclusions* when internal, *blemishes* when external. Flaws can be white, black, colorless, or even red or green in rare instances.

I will discuss some of these flaws here, so that you have a working vocabulary of diamond imperfections.

Internal Flaws or Inclusions

Pinpoint. This is a small, usually whitish dot (although it can be dark) that is difficult to see. There can be a number of pinpoints (a cluster) or a "cloud" of pinpoints (often hazy in appearance and difficult to see).

Dark spot. This may be a small crystal inclusion or a thin, flat inclusion that reflects light like a mirror. It may also appear as a silvery, metallic reflector.

Colorless crystal. This is often a small crystal of diamond, although it may be another mineral. Sometimes it appears very small, sometimes large enough to substantially lower the flaw grade to SI, or even I. A small group of colorless crystals lowers the grade from a possible VS to I_3.

Cleavage. A cleavage is a particular type of crack that has a flat plane that, if struck, could cause the diamond to split, or cleave, as though it had been sliced cleanly with a saw. A large cleavage in the upper part of the diamond can be a serious flaw.

Feather. This is another name for a crack. A small feather is not dangerous and can be a very minor flaw if it does not break through the surface of the stone on the top portion where you might accidentally strike it; a large feather on the top can be a serious flaw.

Bearded girdle or girdle fringes. These are usually the result of hastiness on the part of the cutter while rounding out the diamond. The girdle portion becomes overheated and develops small radial hairlike cracks that resemble small whiskers going into the diamond from the girdle edge. Sometimes the bearding amounts to minimal "peach fuzz" and can be removed with slight repolishing. Sometimes the bearding must be removed by faceting the girdle. If the bearding is very minimal, a diamond can still be graded IF.

Growth or grain lines. These can be seen only when examining the diamond while slowly rotating it. They appear and disappear, usually instantaneously. They will appear in a group of two, three, or four pale brown lines. If they cannot be seen from the crown side of the diamond and are small, they will not affect the grade adversely.

Knaat or twin lines. These are sometimes classified as external flaws because they appear as very small ridges, often with some type of geometrical outline; or as a small, slightly raised dot with a tail resembling a comet. They're difficult to see.

Laser line. Laser techniques are used today to make black flaws less visible, and thus improve the stone aesthetically. Using laser technology, it is possible to "vaporize" black inclusions so they practically disappear. With the loupe, however, an experienced jeweler or gemologist can see the "path" cut into the diamond by the laser beam. This path looks like a fine, straight, white thread starting at the surface of the stone and penetrating into it. See the section on "Clarity Enhancement" later in this chapter.

External Flaws or Blemishes

A natural. A natural is a remnant of the original skin of the diamond, and is often left on the girdle by the cutter in order to get the largest possible diameter from the rough. They are usually seen on the girdle and appear to be a rough, unpolished area. A natural may look like a scratch line or small triangle (called a trigon). If it is no wider than the normal width of the girdle or does not disrupt the circumference of the stone, it may not be considered a blemish. Often naturals are polished and become an extra facet, especially if they occur below the girdle edge.

Nick. This is a small chip, usually on the girdle, and can be caused by an accidental knock or blow in the course of wearing the diamond (especially if the girdle is on the thin side). Sometimes a nick or chip can be seen on the edge where the facets meet. If small, the bruised corner can be polished, creating an extra facet. This usually occurs on the crown.

Girdle roughness. This blemish appears as crisscrossed lines, brighter and duller finishing, and minute chipping. This can be remedied by faceting or repolishing.

Pits or cavities. Pits or holes on the facet. When on the table facet, especially if they are deep, the presence of pits or cavities will quickly lower the grade of the stone. Removing a pit may involve recutting the whole top of the stone and can also shrink the stone's diameter.

Scratch. A scratch is usually a minor defect that can be removed with simple repolishing. Remember, however, that in order to repolish the stone, you must remove it from its setting, and then reset it after it has been polished.

Polishing lines. Many diamonds exhibit polishing lines. If they appear on the pavilion side and are not too obvious, they do not lower the value. In some small diamonds these scratch lines can be obvious and are usually the result of a badly maintained polishing wheel.

Abraded or rough culet. The culet has been chipped or poorly finished. This is usually a minor flaw.

How Does the Clarity Grade
Affect Diamond Value?

I will use the GIA system to explain clarity and its effect on value because it is the most widely used in the United States. As you can see from the comparison chart (on page 61), other systems now use similar classifications. Should you have a diamond with a report from one of these, you can use this chart to find the corresponding GIA grade.

On the GIA scale, FL is the grade given to a stone that has no visible flaws, internal or external, when examined under 10x magnification. Only a highly qualified person will be able to determine this grade. If you are using a loupe as you examine diamonds, remember that it is very difficult for the inexperienced viewer to see flaws that may be readily observable to the experienced jeweler, dealer, or gemologist, and you will not have the experience to determine whether or not a diamond is flawless. Often the novice is unable to see any flaws, even in SI grades, even with use of the loupe. A flawless, colorless, correctly proportioned stone, particularly in a one-carat size or larger, is *extremely* rare and is priced proportionately much higher than any other grade. Some jewelers insist there is no such thing available today.

IF is the grade given to a stone with no internal flaws and with only minor external blemishes that could be removed with polishing, such as nicks, small pits not on the table, and/or girdle roughness. These stones, in colorless, well-proportioned makes, are also rare and are priced proportionately much higher than other grades.

VVS_1 and VVS_2 are grades given to stones with internal flaws that are very, very difficult for a qualified observer to see. These grades are also difficult to obtain and are priced at a premium.

VS_1 and VS_2 are grades given to stones with very small inclusions, difficult for a qualified observer to see. These stones are more readily available in good color and cut, and their flaws will not be visible except under magnification. These are excellent stones to purchase.

SI_1 and SI_2 grades are given to stones with flaws that a qualified observer will see fairly easily under 10x magnification. They are not as rare as the higher grades, so they are less costly; in these grades, flaws may sometimes be visible without magnification when examined from the back side or laterally. These grades are still highly desirable, and since they cannot normally be seen with the naked eye when mounted, they

Flawless   SI₂

No difference can be seen between these two diamonds with the unaided eye, but accurate grading is important because it can dramatically affect price.

may enable one to select a stone with a higher color, or in a larger size, when working with a limited budget.

The *imperfect* grades are given to stones in which flaws may be seen by a qualified observer without magnification; they are readily available and are much less expensive. They are graded I_1, I_2, and I_3. (These grades are called *first piqué* (pronounced pee-kay), *second piqué*, and *third piqué* in some classification systems.) I_1, I_2, and *some* I_3 grades may still be desirable if they are brilliant and lively, and if there are no inclusions that might make them more susceptible than normal to breaking. They should not be automatically eliminated by a prospective purchaser who desires lovely diamond jewelry. As a general rule, however, imperfect grades may be difficult to resell should you ever try to do so.

Exercise Care When Considering a Low Clarity Grade

For those considering a diamond with an I_3 clarity grade, I must issue a word of warning: *some diamonds graded I_3 today are actually industrial quality and not suited for jewelry use.* Some cutters are cutting material that is lower than what is considered acceptable for jewelry. Since there is no grade lower than I_3 at this time, these stones are lumped in with other "better" (jewelry-quality) I_3 stones and are given an I_3 grade as well. But I_3 grade diamonds are *not* all comparable in terms of their clarity, and some should sell for much less than others. Be sure to shop around and compare I_3 diamonds to become familiar with what is acceptable for jewelry use.

Commonly Used Clarity Grading Systems

There are several recognized clarity grading systems in use worldwide, but the system used most widely in the United States and an increasing number of other countries was developed by the GIA. The terms *clarity grade* and *flaw grade* may be used interchangeably, but today the term *clarity* is more commonly used.

The most widely recognized clarity grading scales were introduced by these organizations:

- CIBJO (International Confederation of Jewelry, Silverware, Diamonds, Pearls, and Stones). Participating member nations that use this system include Austria, Belgium, Canada, Denmark, Finland, France, Great Britain, Italy, Japan, Netherlands, Norway, Spain, Sweden, Switzerland, United States, and West Germany
- Scan D.N. (Scandinavian Diamond Nomenclature)
- GIA (Gemological Institute of America)
- AGS (American Gem Society)
- HRD (Hoge Raad voor Diamant, the Diamond High Council of Belgium)

The chart on the following page shows the relationship between the GIA system and others used internationally.

Clarity Enhancement

Today, technological advances have made it possible to improve diamond clarity. Several clarity enhancement techniques are available; some are more or less permanent, and others are definitely not permanent. Unfortunately, clarity enhancement frequently is not disclosed, either to jewelers themselves or by jewelers to their customers. It is important to buy diamonds from knowledgeable, reputable jewelers who check for such treatments. In addition, before buying any diamond, you must *ask* whether or not the stone has been clarity enhanced. If the stone has been enhanced, ask what method was used, and be sure this is stated on the bill of sale. In addition, be sure to ask about special care requirements that might be necessitated by the process.

The two most widely used methods of clarity enhancement are lasering and fracture filling.

Lasering

Laser treatment is used today to make flaws less visible and thus improve the stone aesthetically. Laser technology makes it possible to

Commonly Used Diamond Flaw (Clarity) Grading Systems

CIBJO under 0.47 ct	CIBJO 0.47 ct & over	HRD	SCAN D.N.	GIA	AGS
Loupe clean	Loupe clean	Loupe clean	FL	FL	0
			IF (Internally Flawless	IF	1
VVS	VVS$_1$	VVS$_1$	VVS$_1$	VVS$_1$	
	VVS$_2$	VVS$_2$	VVS$_2$	VVS$_2$	2
VS	VS$_1$	VS$_1$	VS$_1$	VS$_1$	3
	VS$_2$	VS$_2$	VS$_2$	VS$_2$	4
SI	SI$_1$	SI	SI$_1$	SI$_1$	5
	SI$_2$		SI$_2$	SI$_2$	6
Piqué I	Piqué I	P$_1$	1st Piqué	I$_1$ (Imperfect)	7
					8
Piqué II	Piqué II	P$_2$	2nd Piqué	I$_2$	9
Piqué III	Piqué III	P$_3$	3rd Piqué	I$_3$	10

VV = Very, Very   S = Slight or Small
V = Very   I = Inclusion or Included or Imperfect (Imperfection)

For example, VVS may be translated to mean Very, Very Slightly (Included); or Very, Very Small (Inclusion); or Very, Very Slightly (Imperfect). Some jewelers prefer to classify the stone as "very, very small inclusion" rather than "very, very slightly imperfect" because the former description may sound more acceptable to the customer. There is, in fact, no difference.

"vaporize" black inclusions so they practically disappear. With the loupe, however, an experienced jeweler or gemologist can usually see the "path" cut into the diamond by the laser beam—this path may look like a fine, white thread starting at the surface of the stone and traveling into it—and other indicators of lasering. The effects of the laser treatment are permanent. If a lasered diamond is accompanied by a diamond grading report issued by a respected lab, the report will state that the stone is lasered.

A lasered stone should cost less than another with the "same" clarity, so it may be an attractive choice for a piece of jewelry—as long as you *know* it's lasered and therefore pay a fair price for it. You must be sure to ask whether or not the diamond is lasered. Some countries don't require disclosure, and for several years the Federal Trade Commission suspended the requirement to disclose lasering in the United States. This position was reversed—disclosure is now required—but it may take several years for compliance to be restored. If a lab report does not accompany the stone, you must be sure to ask explicitly, and verify it with an independent gemologist-appraiser.

Fracture Filling

Fractures—cracks or breaks—that would normally be visible and detract from the beauty of a diamond can often be filled with a nearly colorless, glasslike substance. After filling, these breaks virtually disappear and will no longer be seen, except under magnification. Filling is *not* a permanent treatment, and special precautions are required when cleaning and repairing jewelry containing a filled diamond. With proper care, such stones may remain beautiful for many years. Careless handling, however, can cause the filler to leave the stone or change color, resulting in a much less attractive diamond. Some filling materials are much more stable than others, but at present it is usually not possible to know what filler has been used in a given stone. Should the filler be accidentally removed, your jeweler can have the treatment repeated to restore the stone's original appearance. The GIA will not issue a grading report on a filled diamond, but other labs will (indicating the grade it appears to be after filling).

Filled diamonds cost much less than other diamonds. They can be a very attractive and affordable alternative as long as you know what you are buying, understand the limitations, and pay the right price. Be sure to ask explicitly whether or not the stone has been fracture-filled, and if the stone does not have a report from a respected lab (see appendix), get a statement *on the bill of sale* as to whether or not it is fracture-filled.

How Does the Position of a Flaw Affect a Diamond's Grading and Value?

As a general rule, the position of any given inclusion will progressively downgrade and devalue a diamond as indicated below:

- *If seen only from the pavilion side,* or seen *clearly* only from the pavilion side, a flaw has the least adverse effect, since it is the least visible from the top.
- *If positioned near the girdle,* while perhaps more visible than described above, a flaw is still difficult to see, and hardly noticeable from the top. Such flaws can be easily covered with the prong of a setting.
- *Under any crown facet* (other than a star facet), a flaw is more easily visible, except when near the girdle.
- *Under a star facet,* a flaw will be much more easily visible.
- *Under the table* is the least desirable position, as it places the flaw where it is most noticeable, and may have the greatest effect on brilliance or fire, depending on the stone's size or color.

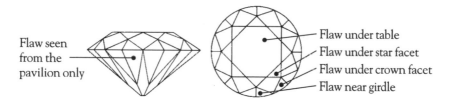

Flaw seen from the pavilion only

Flaw under table
Flaw under star facet
Flaw under crown facet
Flaw near girdle

Sometimes a small black or white flaw may be in such a position that it is reflected within the stone. It may be seen as a reflection to the opposite side of the stone, or, more unfortunately, it may reflect itself as many as *eight times* around the bottom or near the culet of the stone. A diamond with such a flaw might otherwise be classified as a VS$_1$ or VS$_2$, but because of the eightfold reflection resulting from its unfortunate position, the flaw grade will be lowered.

Remember, a diamond does not have to be flawless to be a very fine stone and to have a high value. Personally, I prefer a stone that might be slightly imperfect but has fine color and brilliance over a flawless stone with less sparkle and a less fine color. Color and brilliance are considered the most important factors in terms of a stone's *desirability*. *And remember*: Even a diamond graded I_3 can be beautiful and brilliant.

CHAPTER EIGHT

Weight

What Is a Carat?

Diamonds are sold by the *carat* (ct), not to be confused with *karat* (kt), which in the United States refers to gold purity. Since 1913, most countries have agreed that a carat weighs 200 milligrams, or ⅕ gram.

Before 1913, the carat weight varied depending on the country of origin—usually weighing *more* than the modern carat. The Indian carat didn't weigh the same as the English carat; the French carat was different from the Indian and the English. This is important if you have, or are thinking of buying, a very old piece that still has the original bill of sale indicating carat weight. Since the old carat usually weighed *more* than the post-1913 *metric carat,* an old three-carat stone will often weigh more than three carats by modern standards. Today the term *carat* means the metric carat, the 200-milligram carat with five carats weighing one gram.

What are points? Jewelers often refer to the carat weight of diamonds in terms of *points.* This is particularly true of stones under one carat. There are 100 points to a carat, so if a jeweler says that a stone weighs 75 points, he means it weighs ⁷⁵/₁₀₀ of a carat, or ¾ carat. A 25-point stone is ¼ carat. A 10-point stone is ¹⁄₁₀ carat.

The carat is a unit of weight, not size. I wish to stress this point, since most people think that a one-carat stone is a particular size. Most people, therefore, would expect a one-carat diamond and a one-carat emerald, for example, to look the same size or to have the same apparent dimensions. This is not the case.

Comparing a one-carat diamond with a one-carat emerald and a one-carat ruby easily illustrates this point. First, emerald weighs less than diamond, and ruby weighs more than diamond. This means that a one-carat emerald will look larger than a one-carat diamond, while the ruby will look smaller than a diamond of the same weight. Emerald, with a mineral composition that is lighter, will yield greater mass per carat; ruby, with its heavier composition, will yield less mass per carat.

Let's look at the principle another way. If you compare a one-inch cube of pine wood, a one-inch cube of aluminum, and a one-inch cube of iron, you would easily choose the cube of iron as heaviest, even though it has the same *volume* as the other materials. The iron is like the ruby, while the wood is like the emerald and the aluminum like the diamond. Equal *volumes* of different materials can have very different weights, depending on their density, also called mass or specific gravity.

Equal volumes of materials with the same density, however, should have approximately the same weight, so that in diamond, the carat weight has come to represent particular sizes. These sizes, as I've discussed, are based on diamonds cut to ideal proportions. Consequently, if properly cut, diamonds of the weights given in the chart on page 67 should be approximately the sizes illustrated. Remember, however, *that these sizes will not apply to other gems.*

How Does Carat Weight Affect Value in Diamonds?

Diamond prices are usually quoted *per carat*. Diamonds of the finest and rarest quality are sold for the highest price per carat, and diamonds of progressively less rare quality are sold for a progressively lower price per carat. For example, a rare-quality diamond might sell for $20,000 per carat. So, a stone in this quality weighing 1.12 carats would cost $22,400. On the other hand, a stone of exactly the same weight, in a less rare quality, might sell for only $10,000 per carat, or $11,200.

Also, as a rule, the price increases per carat as we go from smaller to larger stones, since the larger stones are more rare and more limited in supply. For example, stones of the same quality weighing ½ carat will sell for more per carat than stones weighing ⅓ carat; stones weighing ¾ carat will sell for more per carat than stones of the same quality weighing ½ carat. For example, the per carat price of a particular quality ½-carat stone might be $5,000, while the per-carat price for a ⅓-carat stone of the

Sizes and Weights of Various Diamond Cuts

Weight (ct)	Emerald	Marquise	Pear	Brilliant
5				
4				
3				
2½				
2				
1½				
1¼				
1				
¾				
½				

Diameters and Corresponding Weights of Round Brilliant-Cut Diamonds

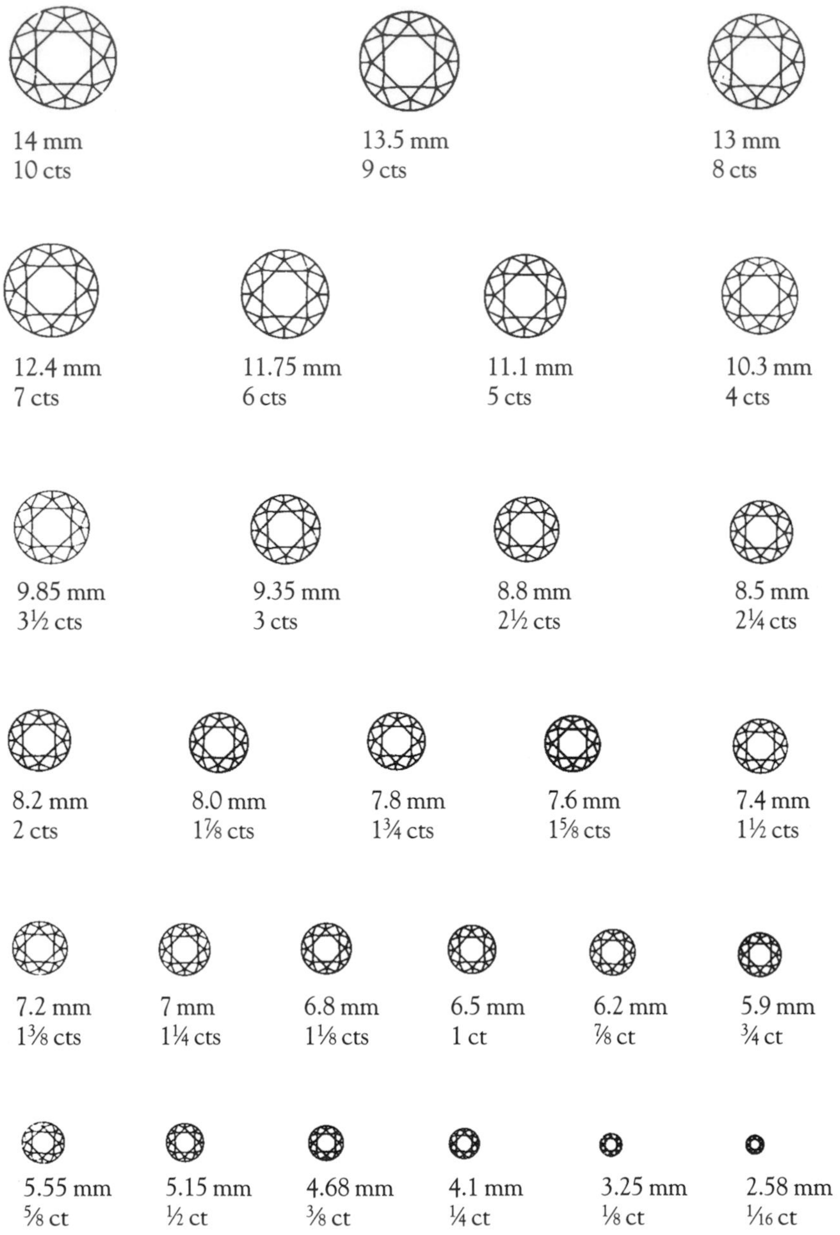

14 mm
10 cts

13.5 mm
9 cts

13 mm
8 cts

12.4 mm
7 cts

11.75 mm
6 cts

11.1 mm
5 cts

10.3 mm
4 cts

9.85 mm
3½ cts

9.35 mm
3 cts

8.8 mm
2½ cts

8.5 mm
2¼ cts

8.2 mm
2 cts

8.0 mm
1⅞ cts

7.8 mm
1¾ cts

7.6 mm
1⅝ cts

7.4 mm
1½ cts

7.2 mm
1⅜ cts

7 mm
1¼ cts

6.8 mm
1⅛ cts

6.5 mm
1 ct

6.2 mm
⅞ ct

5.9 mm
¾ ct

5.55 mm
⅝ ct

5.15 mm
½ ct

4.68 mm
⅜ ct

4.1 mm
¼ ct

3.25 mm
⅛ ct

2.58 mm
1/16 ct

same quality would be $3,000. The stones would cost $2,500 (½ x $5,000) and $1,000 (⅓ x $3,000) respectively.

Furthermore, stones of the same quality weighing exactly one carat will sell for *much* more than stones weighing 90 to 96 points. Thus, if you want a one-carat stone of a particular quality, but you can't afford it, you may find you can afford it in a 95-point stone—and a 95-point stone will give the impression of a full one-carat stone when set. You might be able to get your heart's desire after all.

As you will see, the price of a diamond does not increase proportionately; there are disproportionate jumps. And the larger and finer the stone (all else being equal in terms of overall quality), the more disproportionate the increase in cost per carat may be. A top-quality two-carat stone will not cost twice as much as a one-carat stone; it could easily be *three* times as much. A top-quality five-carat stone would not be five times the cost of a one-carat stone; it could easily be as much as ten times what a one-carat stone might cost.

What Is Spread?

The term *spread* may be used in response to the question "How large is this diamond?" But it can be misleading. Spread refers to the size the stone *appears* to be, based on its diameter. For example, if the diameter of the stone measured the same as you see in the diamond sizes charts (see pages 67 and 68), which represent the diameter of a perfectly proportioned stone, the jeweler might say it "spreads" one carat. But this does not mean it *weighs* one carat. It means it *looks* the same size as a perfectly cut one-carat stone. It may weigh less or more—usually less.

Diamonds are generally weighed before they are set, so the jeweler can give you the exact carat weight, since you are paying a certain price per carat. Remember, also, that the price per carat for a fine stone weighing 96 points is much less than for one weighing one carat or more. So it is unwise to accept any "approximate" weight, even though the difference seems so slight.

As you can see here, it is also important when buying a diamond to realize that since carat refers to weight, the manner in which a stone is cut can affect its apparent size. A one-carat stone that is cut shallow (see chapter 5) will appear larger in diameter than a stone that is cut thick (heavy). Conversely, a thick stone will appear smaller in diameter.

Furthermore, if the diamond has a thick girdle (see chapter 5), the stone will appear smaller in diameter. If this girdle is faceted, it tends to hide the ugly, frosted look of a thick girdle, but the fact remains that the girdle is thick, and the stone suffers because it will appear smaller in diameter than one would expect at a given carat weight. These stones are therefore somewhat cheaper per carat.

CHAPTER NINE

Diamond Grading Reports

Today, few fine diamonds over one carat are sold without a diamond grading report (or certificate, as they are also called) from a respected laboratory. Reports issued by the GIA Gem Trade Laboratory are the most widely used in the United States and in many countries around the world, but reports from other laboratories (see appendix) are also highly respected.

A grading report does more than certify the stone's genuineness; it fully describes the stone and evaluates each of the critical factors affecting quality, beauty, and value. Grading reports can be very useful for a variety of reasons. The information they contain can provide verification of the "facts" as represented by the seller and enable one to make a safer decision when purchasing a diamond. Another important function of reports is to verify the identity of a specific diamond at some future time—if, for example, it has been out of one's possession for any reason. For insurance purposes, the information provided on the report will help ensure replacement of a lost or stolen diamond with one that is truly "comparable quality."

Reports aren't necessary for every diamond, and many beautiful diamonds used in jewelry are sold without them. But when considering the purchase of a very fine diamond weighing one carat or more, I strongly recommend that the stone be accompanied by a report from one of the laboratories listed in the appendix, even if it means having a stone removed from its setting (no reputable lab will issue a full grading report on a mounted diamond) and then reset. If you are considering a stone that lacks a report, it is easy for your jeweler or an appraiser to obtain one.

The availability and widespread use of these reports can, when properly understood, enable even those without professional skills to make valid comparisons between several stones and more informed buying decisions. The key is found in *knowing how to read the reports properly.*

Don't Rely on the Report Alone

Reports can be an important tool to help you understand differences affecting rarity and price. But I must caution you not to let them interfere with what you *like* or really want. Remember, some diamonds are very beautiful even though they don't adhere to established standards. In the final analysis, use your own eyes and ask yourself how you *like* the stone. I had a customer who was trying to decide between several stones. Her husband wanted to buy her the stone with the "best" report, but she preferred another stone which, according to what was on the reports, wasn't as "good." They decided against the "best" stone and bought the one that made her happiest. The important thing is that they knew exactly what they were buying and paid an appropriate price for that specific combination of quality factors. In other words, they made an *informed* choice. The reports gave them assurance as to the facts and greater confidence that they knew what they were really comparing.

Improper Use of Reports Can Lead to Costly Mistakes

As important as diamond grading reports can be, they can also be misused and lead to erroneous conclusions and costly mistakes. The key to being able to rely on a diamond report—and having confidence in your decision—lies in knowing how to read it properly.

When trying to decide between two diamonds accompanied by diamond grading reports, buyers all too often make a decision by comparing just two factors evaluated on the reports—*color* and *clarity*—and think they have made a sound decision. This is rarely the case. No one can make a sound decision based on color and clarity alone. In fact, when significant price differences exist between two stones of the same color and clarity, you will find that often the cheaper stone is *not* the same quality, nor the better value.

Color and clarity provide only part of the total picture and differences in price usually indicate differences in quality that you may not see or understand. With *round* diamonds, *all* the information you need is on the report, but you need to understand what all the information means before you can make valid comparisons.

Properly used, diamond grading reports can give you a more *complete* picture, enable you to make sounder comparisons, and determine who is offering good value. Reading reports may seem complicated at first, but if you take time to learn, and seek the help of a knowledgeable jeweler, you'll be amazed at how much more interesting—and unique— you'll find each diamond will become!

Before beginning, however, I must offer one important word of caution: *Don't make a purchase relying solely on any report without making sure the report matches the stone, and that the stone is still in the same condition described.* Always seek a professional gemologist, gemologist-appraiser, or gem-testing laboratory to confirm that the stone accompanying the report is, in fact, the stone described there, and that the stone is still in the same condition indicated on the report. I know of instances where a report has been accidentally sent with the wrong stone. And, in some cases, deliberate fraud is involved.

Laser Inscription and Ion Beam Technology

Today, some laboratories are routinely providing a laser inscription of the number of the report along the girdle edge of diamonds on which they are issuing reports. This offers some means of ensuring that the stone and report do, in fact, match. If the diamond you are considering does not have a laser inscription, an independent gemologist can confirm that the stone and report match. Should you wish to have the report number inscribed on the girdle, a jeweler or gemologist can make arrangements with a lab for a nominal charge. European Gemological Laboratory, International Gemmological Institute, and the Gemological Institute of America are among the companies providing laser inscription services. In addition to lasering, the International Gemmological Instititute will soon offer a new service that uses ion beam technology to mark a diamond in an innovative manner that is non-invasive and does not mar the diamond in any way. This new technology can also be used to apply a "brand" mark that will be visible only with a special viewer, thus making it more difficult to counterfeit branded diamonds. It will be more difficult to falsify or eradicate such marks as a result of the process itself, so this technology may ultimately replace laser inscriptions.

How to Read a Diamond Grading Report

Check the date issued. It is very important to check the date on the report. It's always possible that the stone has been damaged since the report was issued. This sometimes occurs with diamonds sold at auction. Since diamonds can become chipped or cracked with wear, one must always check them. For example, you might see a diamond accompanied by a report describing it as D–Flawless. If this stone were badly chipped *after the report was issued,* however, the clarity grade could easily drop to VVS, and in some cases, even lower. Needless to say, in such a case, value would be dramatically reduced.

Who issued the report? Check the name of the laboratory issuing the report. Is the report from a laboratory that is known and respected? If not, the information on the report may not be reliable. In the United States, respected laboratories that issue diamond reports include the Gemological Institute of America Gem Trade Laboratory (GIA/GTL), American Gemological Laboratories (AGL), American Gem Society (AGS), Professional Gem Sciences (PGS), and International Gemmological Institute (IGI). Respected European labs issuing diamond reports include the Belgian Diamond High Council (HRD), Laboratory Gubelin (Swiss), and Schweizerische Stiftung fur Edelstein-Forschung (SSEF, Swiss). See the appendix for additional information on these and other laboratories.

Whichever report you are reading (see the end of this chapter for sample reports), all will provide similar information, including:

- *Identity of the stone.* This verifies that the stone is a diamond. Some diamond reports don't make a specific statement about identity because they are called *diamond* reports and are only issued for genuine diamonds. If the report is not called a "diamond grading report," then there must be a statement attesting that the stone described is a genuine diamond.
- *Weight.* The exact carat weight must be given.
- *Dimensions.* Any diamond, of any shape, should be measured and the dimensions recorded as a means of identification, especially for insurance/identification purposes. The dimensions given on a diamond report are very precise and provide information that is important for several reasons. First, the dimensions can help you determine that the diamond being examined is, in fact, the same diamond described in the report, since the likelihood of having two diamonds with exactly the same carat weight and mil-

limeter dimensions is slim. Second, if the diamond has been damaged and recut since the report was issued, the millimeter dimensions may provide a clue that something has been altered, which might affect the carat weight as well. Any discrepancy between the dimensions that you or your jeweler get by measuring the stone, and those provided on the report, should be a red flag to check the stone very carefully.

Finally, the dimensions on the report also tell you whether the stone is *round* or *out-of-round*. Out-of-round diamonds sell for less than those that are more perfectly round. Roundness is explained below in greater detail.

* *Proportioning, finish, girdle thickness, culet, color, and clarity.* These are covered individually on the following pages.

Round, Brilliant-Cut Diamonds Are "Well-Rounded"

In round diamonds, the stone's *roundness* will affect value, so it is determined very carefully from measurements of the stone's diameter, gauged at several points around the circumference. For a round diamond, the report will usually give two diameters, measured in millimeters and noted to the hundredth: for example, 6.51 rather than 6.5; or 6.07 rather than 6.0, and so on. These indicate the highest and the lowest diameter. Diamonds are very rarely perfectly round, which is why most diamond reports will show two measurements. Recognizing the rarity of truly round diamonds, some deviation is permitted, and the stone will not be considered "out-of-round" unless it deviates by more than the established norm, which, in a one-carat stone, is approximately 0.10 millimeter. As the size of a diamond increases, the tolerances also increase.

Acceptable Tolerances for "Round" Diamonds

Weight	Diameter (in mm)	Acceptable Deviation (in mm)
1 ct	6.50	0.10
2 cts	8.20	0.12
3 cts	9.35	0.14
4 cts	10.30	0.16
5 cts	11.10	0.17
10 cts	14.00	0.21

To calculate an acceptable deviation on a particular stone, take the average between the high and low diameter dimensions given; multiply that number by 0.0154. For example, if the dimensions given are 8.20–8.31, the diameter averages 8.25. Multiply 8.25 by 0.0154 = 0.127. The acceptable deviation allowable for this stone will be 0.12– 0.13. The actual deviation in this example is 0.11 (8.31 minus 8.20), well within the tolerance, so this diamond would be "round." Some flexibility is permitted on diamonds over two carats.

Depending on the degree of out-of-roundness, price can be affected by 10 to 15 percent, or much more if the stone is noticeably out-of-round. The greater the deviation, the lower the price should be.

Dimensions for Fancy Shapes

While the dimensions for fancy shapes are not as important as they are for round diamonds, there are length-to-width ratios that are considered "normal" and deviations may result in price reductions of 15 percent or more. The following reflect acceptable ranges:

Pear	1.50:1 to 1.75:1
Marquise	1.75:1 to 2.25:1
Emerald	1.30:1 to 1.60:1
Oval	1.35:1 to 1.70:1

To better understand what this means, let's look at a pear-shaped diamond as an example. If its report showed the length to be 15 millimeters and the width to be 10 millimeters, the length-to-width ratio would be 15 to 10, or 1.50:1. This would be acceptable. If, however, the dimensions were 30 millimeters long by 10 wide, the ratio would be 30 to 10, or 3:1. This would be unacceptable; the ratio is too great, and the result is a stone that looks much too long for its width. A pear-shaped diamond with an unacceptable length-to-width ratio should sell for at least 10 percent less than another pear-shaped diamond. Note: A long pear-shape is not necessarily bad, and some people prefer a longer shape, but it is important to understand that such stones should sell for less than those with "normal" lengths. Always keep in mind the length-to-width ratio of fancy cuts, and adjust the price for stones that are not in the "acceptable" range.

Evaluating Proportioning from the Report

As I discussed earlier, good proportioning is as critical to a diamond as it is to the man or woman who wears it! The proportioning—especially the depth percentage and table percentage—is what determines how much brilliance and fire the stone will have.

The information provided on diamond reports pertaining to proportions is critically important for *round, brilliant-cut diamonds*. Unfortunately, it is only of minimal use with fancy shapes. For fancies, you must learn to rely on your own eye to tell whether or not the proportioning is acceptable: Are there differences in brilliance across the stone? Or flatness? Or dark spots such as "bow ties" resulting from poor proportioning? (See chapter 5.)

Evaluating the proportioning of a diamond is as critical as evaluating the color and clarity grades. Diamonds that are cut close to "ideal" proportions (see chapter 5) and stones with "excellent" makes can easily cost 15 to 25 percent more than a diamond cut with average proportions; diamonds with poor makes sell for 10 to 20 percent less; very badly proportioned stones can be priced as much as 25 to 40 percent less than one with average proportions. As you can see, *the difference in cost between one diamond with "ideal" proportioning and another with "poor"—even where the color and clarity are the same—could be 40 percent or more.* The information on a diamond report can help you evaluate the proportioning and know whether or not you should be paying more, or less, for a particular stone.

"Depth Percentage" and "Table Percentage" Key to Beauty

To determine whether or not a round stone's proportioning is good—which is so critical to its beauty—look at the section of the report that describes *depth percentage* and *table percentage*. The depth percentage represents the depth of the stone—the distance from the table to the culet—as a percentage of the width of the stone. The table percentage represents the width of the table as a percentage of the width of the entire stone. These numbers indicate how well a round stone has been cut in terms of its proportioning, and must adhere to very precise standards. Your eye may be able to see differences in sparkle and brilliance, but you may not be able to discern the subtleties of proportioning. The percentages on the report should fall within a fairly specific range in order for the stone to be judged acceptable, excellent, or poor.

I will not discuss how one calculates these percentages, but it is important for you to know what the ranges are, as outlined in the "Depth Percentage Guidelines" below. Some reports also provide information about the *crown angle*. The crown angle tells you the angle at which the crown portion has been cut. This angle will affect the depth and table percentage. Normally, if the crown angle is between 34 and 36 degrees, the table and depth will be excellent; between 32 and 34, good; between 30 and 32 degrees, fair; and less than 30 degrees, poor. If the exact crown angle is not given, it is probably considered acceptable. If not, there is normally a statement indicating that the crown angle exceeds 36 degrees, or is less than 30 degrees. But once again, use your own eye to determine whether or not you like what you see. I've seen diamonds that are very beautiful despite having angles that are not within the norm.

Depth Percentage

A round diamond cut with a depth percentage between 58 and 64 percent is normally a lovely, lively stone. You should note, however, that girdle thickness will affect depth percentage. A high depth percentage could result from a thick or very thick girdle, so when checking the depth percentage on the diamond report, check the "girdle" information as well.

Stones with a depth percentage over 64 percent or under 57 percent will normally be too deep or too shallow to exhibit maximum beauty and should sell for less. If the depth percentage is too high, the stone will also look smaller than its weight indicates. If the depth percentage is exceptionally high, brilliance can be significantly reduced and a darkish center may also be produced. If the depth percentage is too *low*, brilliance will also be significantly affected. I've seen diamonds that were so shallow—stones with such low depth percentages—that they had no brilliance and liveliness at all. When dirty, such stones look no better than a piece of glass. I avoid stones with depth percentages over 64 percent or under 57 percent. If you are attracted to such stones remember that they should sell for much less per carat.

Depth Percentage Guidelines

Depth Percentage	Effect on Price
Ideal—approximately 58 to 60%	20 to 30% more*
Excellent—60+ to 62%	10 to 20% more*
Good—62 to 64%	————
Fair—64 to 66%	15 to 25% less
Poor—over 66% or less than 57%	20 to 40% less

*For *round* diamonds, combined with the right table percentage and fine overall cutting.

Table Percentage

Round stones cut with tables ranging from 53 to 64 percent usually result in beautiful, lively stones. Diamonds with smaller tables usually exhibit more *fire* than those with larger tables, but stones with larger tables may have more *brilliance*. As you will see, table width affects the stone's personality, but deciding which personality is more desirable is a matter of personal taste.

Table Percentage Guidelines

Table Percentage	Effect on Price
Ideal—from 53 to 58%	20 to 30% more*
Excellent—up to 60% (up to 62% in stones under ½ carat)	10 to 20% more*
Good—to 64%	————
Fair—over 64 to 70%	15 to 30% less
Poor—over 70%	30 to 40% less

*For *round* diamonds, combined with the right depth percentage and fine overall cutting.

Finish

Under *finish* on the diamond report you will find an evaluation of the stone's *polish and symmetry*. Polish serves as an indicator of the care taken by the cutter. The quality of the stone's polish is a factor that cannot be ignored in evaluating the overall quality of a diamond, as well as its cost and value. As with a pair of fine leather shoes, the better the polish, the brighter the surface luster!

Polish can be described on the report as *excellent, very good, good, fair,* or *poor.* The price-per-carat should be less on stones with "fair" or "poor" polish. Cost per carat is usually more for stones that have "very good" or "excellent" polish.

Symmetry describes several factors: (1) how the facet edges align with one another; (2) whether or not the facets from one side of the diamond match corresponding facets on the opposite side; and (3) whether or not facets in the top portion of the diamond are properly aligned with corresponding ones in the bottom portion. When the symmetry is described as "fair"—or worse—something is usually out of line.

When evaluating symmetry, the most important area to check is the alignment of the crown (top) to the pavilion (bottom). If it is not good, it will make a visual difference in the beauty of the stone, and correspondingly in its price. To check for proper alignment here, simply look at the stone from the side to see whether or not the facets just above the girdle align with the facets just beneath the girdle.

When the top and bottom facets don't line up, it indicates sloppy cutting, and, more important, diminishes the overall beauty of the diamond. This will reduce price more than other symmetry faults.

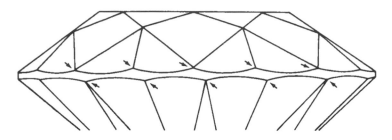

Misalignment of crown and pavilion

How Does the Girdle Affect Value?

The girdle is another important item described on diamond grading reports. The report will indicate whether or not the girdle is polished, or faceted, and how thick it is. Girdle thickness is very important for two reasons: (1) it affects *value* and (2) it affects the stone's *durability.*

Girdle thickness ranges from extremely thin to extremely thick. Diamonds with girdles that are excessively thin or thick normally sell for less than other diamonds. An extremely thin girdle increases the risk of chipping. Remember that despite their legendary hardness, diamonds are brittle, so a very thin edge poses a greater risk.

If a diamond has an extremely thick girdle, its cost should also be reduced somewhat because the stone will look smaller than another diamond of the same weight with a more normal girdle thickness. This is because extra weight is being consumed by the thickness of the girdle itself. (See chapter 8.)

There are some cases in which a very thick girdle is acceptable. Shapes that have one or more points, such as the pear shape, heart, or marquise,

Classic Diamond Shapes

Heart

Marquise

Round Brilliant

Pear

Oval

Emerald Cut

The Shape of Things to Come…

Classic Radiant

Gabrielle® Rectangle

Crisscut®

Royal Asscher®

Gabrielle® Square

Quadrillion™

Lucida™

Context®

...A Blend of Old and New

Gabrielle®
Round

Spirit Sun®

EightStar®
"Super" Ideal

Trilliant

Lily Cut®

Gabrielle® Heart

...And Distinctive Shapes to Accentuate

Briolette

Step-cut lozenge or
kite shape creates
unique elements.

Rondelles

Step-cut half-moons and
trapezoid shapes

Crisscut® baguette and
tapered baguette

Fancy Natural-Color Diamonds...
Rare and Distinctive

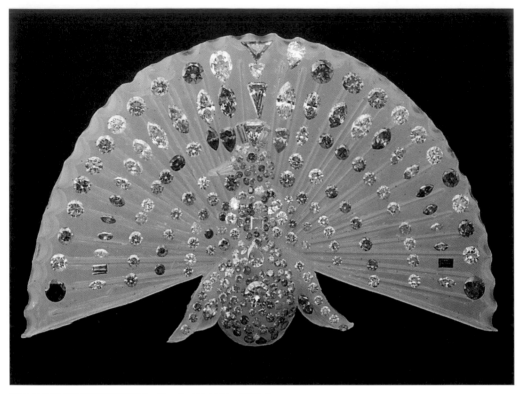

Diamonds occur naturally in more colors and more shades of color than any other gemstone — virtually every color in the rainbow.

…For Jewels that Stand Apart

Rudolf Friedmann's leaf brooch captures the color of Fall with fancy cognac-color diamonds.

Etienne Perret's striking ring with treated-green diamonds

Black and white diamonds, the latest monochromatic trend

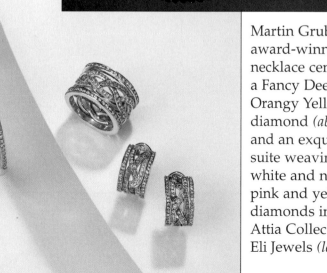

Martin Gruber's award-winning necklace centering a Fancy Deep Orangy Yellow diamond *(above)*, and an exquisite suite weaving white and natural pink and yellow diamonds into the Attia Collection by Eli Jewels *(left)*

Diamonds Sparkle in Contemporary...

Solitaire necklaces
as envisioned by Paul Klecka

Inspired sundial by
John David Cooney

Classic ensemble with contemporary feel
by Robin Garin for Kwiat Couture

Pavé heart pendant, and four-
stone pendant with the feel of a
single stone, create affordable
classics by James Breski.

...And Classic Jewelry

Jewelry using the new Gabrielle® round diamonds

Fanciful hearts by Cheryl Stern *(left)*.

Fancy shapes and fancy colors in the necklace and earrings *(above)* and bracelet *(below)* create memorable jewels by Doron Isaak.

Etienne Perret creates popular line with treated color diamonds.

Whimsical use of fancy-color and colorless diamonds, in bands by Christian Bauer

Diamonds Sparkle Any Time…

Classic elegance using Bellataire™ processed diamonds

Distinctive bracelet using baguette- and princess cut-diamonds by Martin Gruber

Mark Michael bracelet/ring/pendant ensemble captures Art Deco feel with contemporary flourish, while his engagement rings offer a more modern, yet classic look.

Fancy Intense Yellow radiant-cut diamonds framed by round and baguette-cut colorless diamonds by designer Doron Isaak

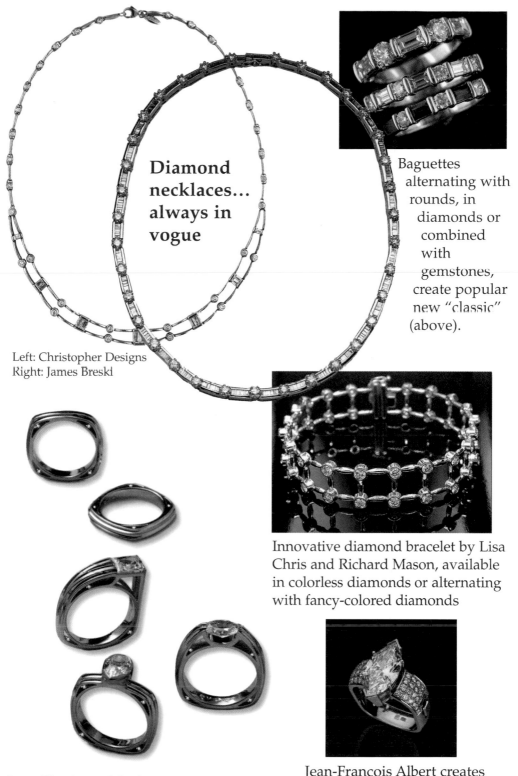

Diamond necklaces… always in vogue

Left: Christopher Designs
Right: James Breski

Baguettes alternating with rounds, in diamonds or combined with gemstones, create popular new "classic" (above).

Innovative diamond bracelet by Lisa Chris and Richard Mason, available in colorless diamonds or alternating with fancy-colored diamonds

Scott Keating adds distinctive diamond "profile accents" in his Viewpoints Collection.

Jean-François Albert creates a contemporary feeling for a classic marquise.

Popular Ring Styles

Three-Stone Rings

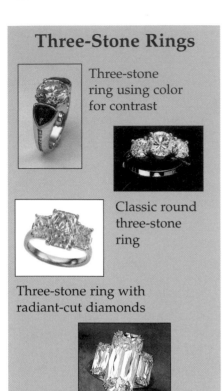

Three-stone ring using color for contrast

Classic round three-stone ring

Three-stone ring with radiant-cut diamonds

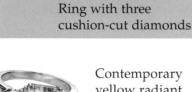

Ring with three cushion-cut diamonds

Three variations of the classic "solitaire"

Classic, yet bold

Solitaire with a "twist"

Classic Tiffany-style six-prong ring

Contemporary yellow radiant cut flanked by trilliants

Old Is New Again

Skilled artisans create intricate "heirloom" reproductions.

Creative Use of Side Stones Enhances the Center

Tiny channel-set stones lead eye to the center.

Classic round with tapered baguettes

Three tapered baguettes on each side of oval

Rare Fancy Vivid Yellow square emerald cut flanked by white trapezoids

Contemporary Bands

Classic bands compliment solitaire by designer Jean-François Albert.

Diamonds encircling the finger: baguette-cut diamonds in channel setting *(left)*; emerald-cut diamonds in bar-set band *(right)*

Band with bar-set emerald-cut diamonds set across top of finger

Bands and stacking rings

Elegant bands with bar-set diamonds

Popular diamond wedding band classics are available in every shape and may be channel-set, bar-set, or prong-set. Equally popular for important anniversary gifts.

Use of contrasting metal textures, black onyx, and diamonds for bold new look for her…or for him

Natural Diamonds in Treated Colors...

Offer a Rainbow of Affordable Hues

Natural diamonds that have been treated by the HPHT annealing process to obtain a "fancy" color

...and Synthetic Diamonds in New Colors, Too

Synthetic diamonds — red, yellow, orange, and blue

can have thick to very thick girdles in the area of the points and still be in the acceptable range. Here the extra thickness in the girdle helps protect the points themselves from chipping.

Generally, a diamond with an extremely thin girdle should sell for less than one with an extremely thick girdle because of the stone's increased vulnerability to chipping. However, if the girdle is much too thick (as in some older diamonds), the price can also be significantly less because the stone can look significantly smaller than other stones of comparable weight.

The Culet

The culet looks like a point at the bottom of the stone, but it is normally another facet—a tiny, flat, polished surface. This facet should be *small or very small*. A small or very small culet won't be noticeable from the top. Some diamonds today are actually pointed. This means that there really is no culet, that the stone has been cut straight down to a point instead. The larger the culet, the more visible it will be from the top. The more visible, the lower the cost of the stone. Stones described as having a large or "open" culet, as in old-European or old-mine cut diamonds (see chapter 5), are less desirable because the appearance of the culet causes a reduction in sparkle or brilliance at the very center of the stone. For the same reasons, a chipped or broken culet will seriously detract from the stone's beauty and significantly reduce the cost.

Color and Clarity Grades

The color and clarity grades found on a diamond report are the items with which most people are familiar, and I have already discussed them in detail in chapters 6 and 7. They are important factors in terms of determining the value of a diamond, but as the preceding discussion has shown, they do not tell the whole story.

The placement, number, type, and color of internal and external flaws will be indicated on a diamond report (note "Key to Symbols" on a GIA report), and may include a plotting—a diagram showing all the details. Be sure you carefully note *all* the details in addition to the cumulative grade. Remember, the *placement* of imperfections can affect value (see chapter 7). You should pay special attention to the section that says "Key to Symbols." This is where lasering will be indicated if the diamond is lasered. This means that the clarity grade indicated is *after* lasering. Its cost should be 15 to 20 percent less than another diamond with the "same" clarity grade. With regard to *fracture filling,* a reliable diamond grading report cannot be issued on a fracture-filled diamond so most laboratories will not grade diamonds that have been clarity enhanced by this method. Most will return the stone *ungraded,* with a notation that it is fracture-filled. Some labs will provide a "qualified" clarity grade, indicating it is fracture-filled and that the grading cannot be precise.

A Word About Fluorescence

Fluorescence, if present, will also be indicated on a diamond grading report (see chapter 6). It will be graded *faint, weak, moderate, strong,* or *very strong.* Some reports indicate the color of the fluorescence (blue, yellow, white, and so on). If the fluorescence is moderate to very strong and the color is not indicated, you should ask the jeweler to tell you what color the stone fluoresces. A stone with strong yellow fluorescence should sell for less since it will appear more tinted when worn in daylight or fluorescent lighting. The presence of blue fluorescence will not detract and in some cases may be considered a bonus, since it may make the stone appear whiter than it really is when seen in daylight or fluorescent lighting. However, if the report shows a *very strong* blue fluorescence, be sure to view the stone in daylight or fluorescent light to see whether or not there is an oily or murky appearance to the diamond. If so, it should sell for less; if not, then value should not be affected.

Pay Attention to "Comments"

On the GIA diamond grading report, and on most other reports issued by major laboratories, there is a section under which additional comments are provided. What is worth noting here is important, and you should be sure you understand what the comment is telling you. Here you will find comments on characteristics such as the presence of "graining" (see page 56). Graining may not affect the appearance or value of a stone at all, but sometimes graining can reduce brilliance, so you should look more closely at the stone to make sure it doesn't affect its beauty. Here you will also find special notations regarding "crown" or "pavilion" angles, indicating that the angle at which the upper or lower portion of the stone has been cut may be less than or greater than the norm. Here again, you must look carefully at the stone to be sure its beauty has not been diminished by faulty cutting. And last, but not least, this is where you will find any notation regarding certain treatments, such as clarity enhancement or the new high-pressure/high-temperature (HPHT) process used to enhance diamond color; if the laboratory issues a report on a diamond that has been treated in some manner, the presence of some type of enhancement will be noted under "Comments."

A Final Word About Reports

Diamond grading reports provide a very useful tool to aid in comparing diamonds and evaluating quality and value. But the key to their usefulness is proper understanding of how to read them.

Today we are seeing new diamond reports accompanying diamonds and diamond jewelry that are *not* as in-depth as the full "diamond *grading* reports" issued by major laboratories. While they provide a briefer and less detailed description or identification of the diamond, and do not usually include a clarity plotting, they do serve a useful purpose and help retailers provide greater assurance to customers regarding the quality of the stones they are selling, at a more reasonable cost than doing a full report. For smaller diamonds or diamonds that are already set in jewelry, these documents are more practical. Among this new genre you will see the GIA's *Diamond Dossier*® that is issued for diamonds weighing 0.18 to 0.99 carats, the International Gemmological Institute's *Diamond Identification Report*, and the European Gemological Laboratory's *Gem Passport*, which they will issue with mounted diamonds (which may be necessary when it is not possible or practical to remove stones from a setting).

For fine-quality diamonds weighing one carat or more, I highly recommend a full diamond grading report, even if it means removing the stone from the setting—even if it already has a limited document such as those discussed in the preceding paragraph.

Take time to learn and understand what *all* the information on the report really means, as well as differences in the type and quality of information provided. When you do, you will really understand what you are buying, and make a wiser choice.

GIA GEM TRADE LABORATORY

A Division of GIA Enterprises, Inc.
A Wholly Owned Subsidiary of the Nonprofit Gemological Institute of America, Inc.

10012345

580 Fifth Avenue
New York, New York 10036-4794
(212) 221-5858
FAX: (212) 575-3095

5355 Armada Drive
Carlsbad, California 92008-4699
(760) 603-4500
FAX: (760) 603-1814

FEB 02 1998

DIAMOND GRADING REPORT

THE FOLLOWING WERE, AT THE TIME OF THE EXAMINATION, THE CHARAC-
TERISTICS OF THE DIAMOND DESCRIBED HEREIN BASED UPON 10×
MAGNIFICATION (FULLY CORRECTED TRIPLET LOUPE AND BINOCULAR
MICROSCOPE), DIAMONDLITE AND MASTER COLOR COMPARISON
DIAMONDS, ULTRAVIOLET LAMPS, MILLIMETER GAUGE, CARAT BALANCE,
PROPORTIONSCOPE, AND ANCILLARY INSTRUMENTS AS NECESSARY.

RED SYMBOLS DENOTE INTERNAL CHARACTERISTICS (INCLUSIONS).
GREEN SYMBOLS DENOTE EXTERNAL CHARACTERISTICS (BLEMISHES).
SYMBOLS INDICATE TYPE, POSITION AND APPROXIMATE SIZE OF
CHARACTERISTICS. DETAILS OF FINISH ARE NOT SHOWN. DIAGRAM MAY
BE APPROXIMATE.

KEY TO SYMBOLS
∘ CRYSTAL
⌐ FEATHER
· PINPOINT
∧ NATURAL

SHAPE AND CUTTING STYLE .. ROUND BRILLIANT

Measurements .... 6.90 - 6.97 X 4.20 MM.

Weight .... 1.25 CARATS

PROPORTIONS ...

Depth .... 60.6 %

Table .... 61 %

Girdle .... MEDIUM TO SLIGHTLY THICK, FACETED

Culet .... VERY SMALL

FINISH

Polish .... VERY GOOD

Symmetry ..... VERY GOOD

CLARITY GRADE .. VS1

COLOR GRADE ... F

Fluorescence ..... NONE

COMMENTS:

"GIA 10012345" has been inscribed on the girdle of this diamond.

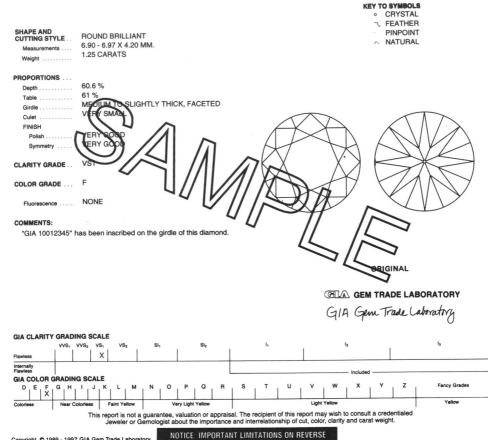

ORIGINAL

GIA GEM TRADE LABORATORY

GIA Gem Trade Laboratory

GIA CLARITY GRADING SCALE

	VVS₁	VVS₂	VS₁	VS₂	SI₁	SI₂	I₁	I₂	I₃
Flawless			X						
Internally Flawless							Included		

GIA COLOR GRADING SCALE

D	E	F	G	H	I	J	K	L	M	N	O	P	Q	R	S	T	U	V	W	X	Y	Z	Fancy Grades
		X																					
Colorless			Near Colorless			Faint Yellow			Very Light Yellow						Light Yellow									Yellow

This report is not a guarantee, valuation or appraisal. The recipient of this report may wish to consult a credentialed
Jeweler or Gemologist about the importance and interrelationship of cut, color, clarity and carat weight.

Copyright © 1989 - 1997 GIA Gem Trade Laboratory

NOTICE: IMPORTANT LIMITATIONS ON REVERSE

GIA reports do not give a cut grade. Note laser inscription under "Comments" section.

American Gemological Laboratories ™   Diamond Grading Report

580 Fifth Avenue
Suite 706
New York, N.Y. 10036
Tel: (212) 704-0727
Fax: (212) 704-7614

DOCUMENT NO: 543 / 601 - 1 (DUPLICATE)

DATE: 25 June, 2001

SHAPE AND CUT: Square Emerald Cut

CARAT WEIGHT: 10.349 Cts.

MEASUREMENTS: 12.48 x 12.25 x 8.38 mm.

PROPORTIONS   Very Good - Good (3 - 4)

Depth %:   68.4%
Table Diameter %:   57.1%
Girdle Thickness: Medium - Faceted
FINISH GRADE: Good (4 - 5)

CLARITY GRADE: AGL: Fl (Free of Inclusions)
(10X Magnification)

COLOR GRADE: AGL: Natural Blue (Exceptional)
UV Fluorescence   None   GIA Color Grade: Fancy Vivid Blue.

COMMENTS: "GIA Clarity Grade: VVS₂; "Total Quality Integration Rating: Exceptional; "Minor details of finish and non-identifying features not plotted. "The image contained in this document is for representational purposes only and is not necessarily actual color or size.

Color Scale (GIA)	D/E	F/G	H/I	J/K	L	M	N	O	P/Q	R	S through Z	Z+
	Color-less	Near Colorless		Faint Yellow			Very Light Yellow			Light Yellow		Fancy Yellow

Clarity Scale (GIA)	F	IF	VVS₁	VVS₂	VS₁	VS₂	SI₁	SI₂	I₁	I₂	I₃

Cutting/Finish (AGL)	1	2	3	4	5	6	7	8	9	10
	Excellent	Very Good		Good			Fair			Poor

This report prepared by:

AGL ™

American Gemological Laboratories, Inc.   Original

© 1976 American Gemological Laboratories, Inc.

AGL reports describe the cut and finish and provide a numerical grade.

Cut Scale	AGS	0	1	2	3	4	5	6	7	8	9	10
		AGS Ideal	AGS Excellent	AGS Very Good	AGS Good			AGS Fair			AGS Poor	

Color Scale	AGS	0	0.5	1.0	1.5	2.0	2.5	3.0	3.5	4.0	4.5	5.0	5.5	6.0	6.5	7.0	7.5	8.0	8.5	9.0	9.5	10.0	To	Fancy Yellow
	GIA	D	E	F	G	H	I	J	K	L	M	N	O	P	Q	R	S	T	U	V	W	X	Y	Z	Fancy Yellow
		COLORLESS			NEAR COLORLESS				FAINT YELLOW			VERY LIGHT YELLOW				LIGHT YELLOW							

Clarity Scale	AGS	0	1	2	3	4	5	6	7	8	9	10
	GIA	FLAWLESS / IF	VVS1	VVS2	VS1	VS2	SI1	SI2	I1	I2	I3	

Key to Symbols

Bruise	×	Crystal	O	Laser Drill Hole	⊕
Cavity	⊘	Extra Facet	∧	Natural	∧
Chip	∧	Feather	∿	Needle	∕
Cleavage	≈	Indented Natural	⩘	Pinpoint	•
Cloud	⋰	Knot	⊙	Twinning Wisp	∿

AGS reports provide a cut grade. Note the scale they use to indicate the quality of cutting.

SOURCE: AMERICAN GEM SOCIETY LABORATORIES

certificate no.   000000000

The HRD Certificates Department is BELTEST accredited for the quality examination of polished diamonds under ref. N° 047.

This certificate is established in conformity with the "International Rules for Grading Polished Diamonds", approved by the World Federation of Diamond Bourses and the International Diamond Manufacturers Association at the May 1978 Congress (rev. ed 1995), and may not be reproduced by any means whatsoever unless complete.

The stone in accordance with the above mentioned number has been identified as a natural gem diamond and has the following description :

shape	brilliant
weight	1.02 ct
clarity grade	loupe-clean
fluorescence	nil
colour grade	exceptional white (E)
measurements	6.58-6.64mm x 3.89mm
proportions	very good
girdle	thin 2.5%
culet	pointed
table width	63%
cr. height	12.5%
pav. depth	44%
finish grade	very good
comments	

antwerpen, 11/03/1996

gemmologists

The characteristics of the above mentioned diamond have been established by scientific measurements and observations, carried out in the laboratory of the Diamond High Council.

clarity grade
(magnification 10 ×)

loupe-clean	X
vvs 1	
vvs 2	
vs 1	
vs 2	
si 1	
si 2	
p 1	
p 2	
p 3	

colour grade

exceptional white +	
exceptional white	X
rare white +	
rare white	
white	
slightly tinted white	
tinted white	
tinted colour	

proportions

very good	X
good	
unusual	

finish grade

very good	X
good	
medium	
poor	

identification marks :
negligible external characteristics

Red symbols refer to internal and green symbols to external characteristics. The symbols do not usually reflect the actual size of the characteristics. The characteristics have been indicated in order to clarify the description and/or for further identification.

HRD describes the quality of the cut and finish.

SOURCE: HOGE RAAD VOOR DIAMANT (THE DIAMOND HIGH COUNCIL OF BELGUIM)

LON 0091285

The Gem Testing Laboratory of Great Britain

LONDON DIAMOND REPORT

Carat weight: 2.30

Colour grade: F RARE WHITE +

Clarity grade: VVS 2

Shape and cutting style: ROUND BRILLIANT

Measurements: 9.06 - 9.13 x 5.16 mm

Proportions: Height: 56.7%

Table: 68 %

Polish: VERY GOOD

Symmetry: GOOD

Girdle: VERY THIN TO THIN

UV-fluorescence: FAINT

Comments:

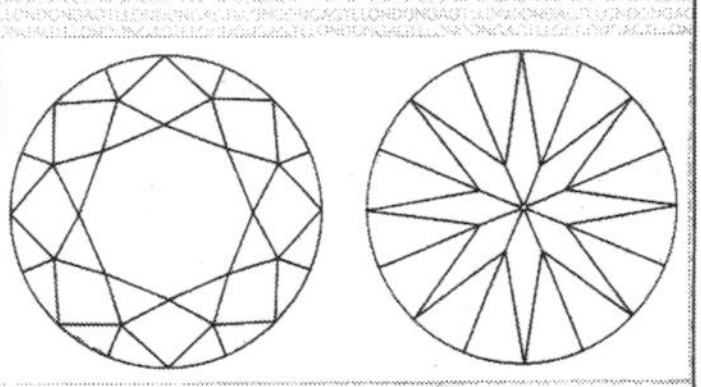

This Report does not make any statement with respect to the monetary value of the diamond.
Only the original report with signature and embossed stamp is a valid identification document.

The Gem Testing Laboratory of Great Britain is the official CIBJO recognised Laboratory for Great Britain.

The Gem Testing Laboratory of Great Britain

GAGTL, 27 Greville Street,
London, ECIN 8SU, Great Britain

Telephone: +44 171 405 3351
Fax: +44 171 831 9479

Signed SAMPLE

Date 22nd May 2001

No cut grade is provided although essential information pertaining to cutting is given.

SOURCE: THE GEM TESTING LABORATORY OF GREAT BRITAIN

PROFESSIONAL GEM SCIENCES

An Independent Laboratory for the
Study and Grading of Diamonds and Gemstones

5 S. Wabash Avenue, Suite 1905
Chicago, IL 60603
Phone (312) 920-1541
Fax   (312) 920-1547

•

550 S. Hill Street, Suite 1595
Los Angeles, CA 90013
Phone (213) 622-2387
Fax   (213) 622-3138

•

Toll Free (800) 235-3287

www.progem.com

CERTIFICATE OF QUALITY

IDENTIFICATION

Species	Natural Diamond	Report Number	XdSAMPLE
Variety	Diamond	Date	May 08, 2001
Shape & Cut	Round Brilliant Cut		
Carat Weight	0.75 ct.	Precision Weight	0.7565 ct.
Clarity Grade*	VS1	Graining	Nil
Color Grade**	F	Fluorescence	Very Faint

Clarity Representation

Internal Characteristics are shown in red. External Characteristics are shown in green. Extra facets are shown in black. Symbols indicate the position of identifying characteristics, not necessarily their size. Hairline feathers in the girdle, minor bearding, and minor details of polish and finish are not shown.

KEY TO SYMBOLS

Feather		Crystal	
Cloud		Natural	

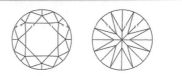

CUT INFORMATION

Dimensions	5.78 - 5.87 x 3.62 mm.	Total Depth	62.1%
Table Width	56%		
	Crown Angle 35.5°	Crown Height	16.0%*
	Pavilion Angle 40.5°	Pavilion Depth	43.0%*
Girdle Thickness	Thin to Slightly Thick, Frosty, Smooth	Average	3.1%*
		*TOTAL	62.1%
Culet Size	Small, Polished (1.0%)		

FINISH

Polish	Very Good to Excellent
Symmetry	Good to Very Good

COMMENTS

Ideal Cut.   Additional pinpoints not shown.

* Clarity grade determined at 10x magnification with a corrected loupe.
** Color grade determined by comparison to approximately 1 carat size, master comparison diamonds.
*** Color Analysis determined by comparison to Munsell color order standards as presented in the book *The World of Color*.

Note: Please read the important limitations to this report printed on the reverse side.

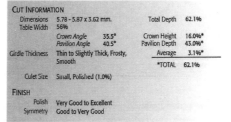

Security Control Number

SAMPLE

QUALITY CONTROL By:

Thomas E. Tashey Jr.

Thomas E. Tashey, Jr., G.G., F.G.A.

©2001 PGS, INC

This report provides a cut grade in the "Comments" section.
Here the cut is graded "ideal."

INTERNATIONAL GEMMOLOGICAL INSTITUTE

DIAMOND IDENTIFICATION REPORT

REPORT NUMBER: SAMPLE   **DATE:** 1/22/1999

SHAPE AND CUTTING STYLE   ROUND BRILLIANT CUT

Measurements: 6.40 - 6.40 x 3.85 MM.

CARAT WEIGHT: 1.01 CARATS

CUT PROPORTIONS

   Depth: 60.0 %

   Table: 60 %

   Girdle: MEDIUM, FACETED

   Culet: NONE

FINISH

    Polish: VERY GOOD

    Symmetry: VERY GOOD

CLARITY GRADE: VS I

COLOR GRADE: D (0+)

   Fluorescence: NONE

COMMENTS: "IGI MILLENNIUM"

       Laserscribed on the girdle.

COPYRIGHT© 1998 I.G.I.

"IGI MILLENNIUM"

The gemstone described in this Identification Report ("Report") has been graded, tested, analyzed, examined and/or inscribed by International Gemological Institute ("I.G.I.") I.G.I. employs and utilizes those techniques and equipment currently available to I.G.I., including, without limitation, 10X magnification corrected triplet loupe and binocular microscope, master color comparison diamonds, non-contact-optical measuring device, and such other instruments and/or processes as deemed appropriate by I.G.I. This Report includes advanced security features. A duly accredited gemologist or jeweler can advise you with respect to the importance of and interrelationship between cut, color, clarity and carat weight. **THIS REPORT IS NEITHER A GUARANTEE, VALUATION NOR APPRAISAL OF THE GEMSTONE DESCRIBED HEREIN. *PLEASE REVIEW THE LIMITATIONS AND RESTRICTIONS SET FORTH ON THE BACK OF THIS REPORT.***

CLARITY SCALE

FLAWLESS / INTERNALLY FLAWLESS	VERY, VERY SLIGHTLY INCLUDED		VERY SLIGHTLY INCLUDED		SLIGHTLY INCLUDED		INCLUDED		
	VVS$_1$	VVS$_2$	VS$_1$	VS$_2$	SI$_1$	SI$_2$	I$_1$	I$_2$	I$_3$

COLOR SCALE

COLORLESS			NEAR COLORLESS				FAINT		VERY LIGHT				LIGHT									FANCY COLOR
D	E	F	G	H	I	J	K	L	M	N	O	P	Q	R	S	T	U	V	W	X	Y	Z

This Diamond *Identification* Report provides useful information but is not as detailed as a *grading* report. Note that there is no clarity plotting. Under "Comments" you will also see that a laser inscription is indicated.

CHAPTER TEN

False Claims & Costly Bargains:
How to Spot Fraud and Avoid Misrepresentation

A s you have seen, many factors affect quality and value in diamonds. When the average person is looking at a stone already set, it is very difficult, if not impossible, to *see* differences that can dramatically affect cost. For this reason, I recommend buying any important diamond *unmounted,* and mounting it only after all the facts have been verified. But you don't have to be a gemologist or fear buying jewelry. Anyone who follows a few simple steps can buy with confidence.

Four Key Steps to Avoiding Fraud or Misrepresentation

- *The first step is to buy from someone both accessible and knowledgeable.* Sellers should have the skill to know for sure what they themselves are buying and selling. This is not to say that there aren't bargains to be found in flea markets, estate sales, and so on, but you run a higher risk when purchasing in such places because of possible misinformation, intentional or otherwise. You must weigh the risk versus the potential reward. In addition, before making a final purchasing decision, ask yourself whether or not you will be able to find the seller again if what you bought turns out to be other than represented. This is equally true when you are traveling and are considering a jewelry purchase abroad.

  Keep in mind that unless the jeweler also does business in the country where you live, it may be cost prohibitive to try to rectify any misrepresentation if it occurs.

- *Second, ask the right questions.* Don't be afraid to ask direct, even pointed questions. The key to getting complete information about what you are buying is asking good questions so you can be sure you are aware of important factors affecting quality and value. (To help you ask the right questions, I provide a complete list in chapter 14.)
- *Third, get the facts in writing.* Be sure the seller is willing to put *in writing* the answers to the questions you ask, and any representations made about the gem or jewelry you are considering. If not, I recommend against purchasing from this seller unless there is an unconditional return policy that allows merchandise to be returned within a reasonable period of time for a full refund (not a store credit). In this case, follow the next step to be safe.
- Finally, *verify the facts with a gemologist-appraiser.* It's especially important to verify whatever has been put in writing with a professional gemologist-appraiser (see chapter 17). Some unscrupulous dealers are willing to put anything in writing to make the sale, knowing that written assurances or claims about the stone are often sufficient to satisfy buyers' doubts. So this last step may be the most important to ensure that you make a wise decision.

In general, you need not worry about fraud or misrepresentation, whether deliberate or unintentional, if you simply follow these four easy steps. They may require a little more time and nominal additional expense, but the end result will be greater knowledge—and assurance—about your jewelry choice and your jeweler. And, they may save you from a costly mistake.

Types of Misrepresentation
Beware of Bargains!

Diamonds Represented to Be Better Than They Are

Beware of bargains. Most are not. When a price seems too good to be true, it usually is, unless the seller doesn't know its true value (which reflects badly on the seller's expertise).

A large jewelry store in Philadelphia was recently found guilty of misrepresenting the quality of diamonds it was selling. Sales staff consistently represented their diamonds to be several color grades and/or flaw grades better than they actually were. As a result, their prices seemed much more attractive than those of other jewelers. Customers thought they were getting a much better buy from this firm than from others in the area, which may not have been the case; since customers didn't know the true quality of the stones they were buying, they couldn't make a fair comparison with what other jewelers were offering. Other jewelers in the area were, in fact, giving better value on stones comparable to what was actually being sold by this "bargain" firm.

Such firms can be found in every city. Many are even willing to put everything in writing, often including a full "appraisal." Such dishonest practices often go undetected because most people assume that when a seller is willing to "put it in writing," he or she is properly representing the item. Most buyers never bother to have the facts verified.

Are Wholesale Prices Really Wholesale?

It is natural to be lured by the promise of getting a diamond at a wholesale price: a price significantly below what most retailers charge. I've already discussed some of the pitfalls, but many fall into the trap of believing that even if they don't get exactly what they are told, they will still get it at a price below what they might have paid at a local jewelry store. Yet, this is frequently not the case.

I recently went undercover for one of the TV networks and made a purchase from a diamond dealer touting "wholesale" prices. In addition to misrepresentation of quality, the price I paid for the diamond was *double* the stone's *retail* value. I purchased a stone described by the seller to have a color grade of J–K and a clarity grade of SI_2. He gave me an appraisal with all the representations stated clearly in writing. The diamond was actually X-color, and the clarity was no better than "I_2." It was also fracture-filled, despite the fact that he had shown me fracture-filled diamonds, explaining what they were—and supposedly gaining my confidence by so doing—and I had told him explicitly that I did not want a fracture-filled diamond! I paid $3,200 for the stone; the *retail* value was $1,400 to $1,500. I could have purchased this stone from any retail jeweler for less. The moral: don't assume you get a good buy just because you are in a "wholesale" jewelry district.

Scams Involving "Appraisals" Prior to Sale

Beware of jewelers who are not willing to put the facts in writing but who offer to let you take the stone, before the sale, to an appraiser in the neighborhood. This may be a scam. It is often seen in wholesale districts like New York's famous 47th Street.

The first step in this scam is to build you up with all the reasons why you are going to get an exceptional buy because the seller "bought it right" (whatever that means), or wants to "pass the savings on to you," or, isn't greedy ("I don't care who I sell to at wholesale; after all, a sale is a sale"), and so on. When you find something you are seriously interested in buying, the seller then explains, for a variety of seemingly valid reasons, why he or she will not put any information pertaining to the quality of the stone in writing, on the bill of sale. The salesperson offers to permit you to go with one of the firm's "bonded guards" to a local appraiser so that you can verify the facts and learn for yourself what a bargain you are getting. Many people are immediately hooked, and conclude erroneously that since they can get an appraisal if they choose, everything must be in order. So they don't. And they become the victims of intentional misrepresentation.

Those who do wish to get an appraisal usually face another problem. They don't know any appraiser—or certainly not any in the neighborhood. Many visitors to 47th Street, for example, are from out of town and don't know anyone local. Unscrupulous sellers often count on this because it gives them the opportunity to recommend several "reliable" appraisers. Or, rather than be so obvious, they suggest you "choose" your own (some even make a fuss about not wanting to know whom you choose). Many purchasers make a big mistake here because they don't realize that *all appraisers are not the same, nor are all appraisers equally competent or reliable* (see chapter 17). Unfortunately, the "reliable appraiser" in this situation often means that the seller can rely on the appraiser to tell the prospective buyers what the seller wants them to hear.

One must always be careful of recommendations from the seller. While legitimate jewelers usually know better than anyone else who the best gemologist-appraisers are in their communities, and their recommendations should be respected, you must still be sure to check the credentials yourself to avoid such scams. Unfortunately, especially in the jewelry districts of major cities, far too many appraisers are not qualified, and some are in collusion with unscrupulous jewelers.

One of my clients had an experience that provides an excellent example of how this type of scam can work. She went to a 47th Street firm in New York. She was offered a five-plus carat diamond ring at a price that was one-fourth the price most retailers had been quoting for what appeared to be comparable quality. She thought the ring looked very beautiful and became very excited about being able to get such a bargain. But when she asked the seller if he would back up his description of the quality of the diamond in writing, he said it was against his store policy, but he would be happy for her to take the ring to a neighborhood appraiser before she purchased it.

This made her cautious, especially since she didn't know any local appraiser. Luckily, I was in New York at the time and was able to use a colleague's lab to examine the ring carefully (it was awkward for the seller to refuse). Not surprisingly, the quality was not as represented. The flaw grade had been misrepresented by *four* grades, and the color had been enhanced *seven grades* by "painting" (painted diamonds have a coating that doesn't come off with normal cleaning and may take months or years to wear off). We had to clean the stone chemically to determine that it was painted and to reveal its true color!

In this particular case, given the true value of the diamond, the price being asked for the ring was certainly not the "steal" it appeared to be. It wasn't a bad price, but other retailers were offering comparable stones at comparable prices or less.

Such practices are overtly dishonest, of course, but all too often they leave honest jewelers in a bad light as a result. In such cases, the dishonest jeweler will appear to be offering the best price, while the honest jeweler—who may actually be offering the best value—falsely appears to be charging "too much."

In general, you need to guard against fraud or misrepresentation in one of the following four areas:

- Weight misrepresentation
- Color alteration and misgrading
- Flaw concealment and misgrading
- Certification—alteration and counterfeit certificates

Weight

Giving "total weight" of all stones where more than one is involved, rather than the exact weight of the main stone, is another form of misrepresentation. This is in strict violation of Federal Trade Commission rulings. When the weight is given, particularly on any display card, descriptive tag, or other type of advertising for a particular piece of jewelry, the weight of the main stone or stones should be clearly indicated as well as the total weight of all the stones.

Thus, if you purchase a "three-carat diamond" ring with one large center stone and two small side stones (as found in many engagement rings), the center stone's weight should be clearly stated; for example, "The weight of the center stone is 2.80 carats, with side stones that weigh 0.10 carats each, for a total weight of 3.00 carats." There is a tremendous price difference between a single stone weighing three carats and numerous stones having a total weight of three carats. A single three-carat stone of good quality could sell for $50,000, while three carats consisting of numerous stones (even with some weighing as much as a carat or more) of the same quality could sell anywhere from $5,000 to $20,000, depending on how many there are and the weight of each.

When inquiring about the weight of a diamond, don't ask the wrong question. Usually the jeweler will be asked how *large* the stone is, rather than how much it *weighs*. In any case, the answer should provide the exact carat weight. Beware when the response includes the word spread: "this stone *spreads* one carat." *A stone that spreads one carat does not weigh one carat;* it simply *looks* like a one-carat stone in its width.

Color

Failure to Disclose Permanent Treatments

Diamonds can be treated in many ways to improve their color. Some are temporary and others are permanent. Regardless of permanence, any treatment should be disclosed so that you know you are paying an appropriate price.

High-pressure/high-temperature annealing (HPHT). This is a new treatment being used to enhance diamonds. The process can transform very tinted, off-white diamonds (as low as Q–Z colors) into colorless and near-colorless stones—even D, E, and F! It can also be used to create fancy colors (see chapter 6). Fancy colors include greenish yellow, yellowish green, and even very rare shades of pink and blue. The change is permanent, but detection requires sophisticated equipment that can be found only in major gem-testing laboratories.

Diamonds treated by HPHT annealing entered the marketplace before the gemological community was aware of the use of this technology on diamonds and before they understood how to distinguish them from natural diamonds. *I recommend that any colorless or near-colorless diamond that has a diamond report issued between January 1996 and June 2000 be examined by a gemologist to determine whether or not it is one of the rare diamond types that respond to this treatment and, if so, that it be resubmitted to a major gem-testing lab (see appendix) for verification.*

Fancy-color diamonds produced by the HPHT annealing process, especially pink and blue diamonds, are more difficult to detect and involve several diamond types. So having a gemologist confirm whether or not the stone is one of the rare types used to produce colorless stones will not be useful. I highly recommend that fancy-color blue and pink diamonds purchased recently be accompanied by a lab report issued by a major lab, and that if a report already accompanies the stone, that it be resubmitted if the report predates December 2000.

Radiation treatment. Exposing off-color diamonds such as yellowish or brownish tinted stones (and also badly flawed stones in which the flaws would be less noticeable against a colored background) to certain types of radiation can result in the production of fancy-colored stones. This treatment produces rich yellows, greens, and blues, and greatly enhances salability because these colors are very desirable. In and of itself, radiation is not fraud; in fact, it may make a "fancy" color diamond affordable to someone otherwise unable to afford one. But again, just be sure that the stone is properly represented and you know what you are buying, and that you are getting it at the right price—which should be much lower than that of the natural fancy.

Temporary Color Enhancement

Touching the culet with ink. Touching the culet, or side, of a slightly yellow stone with a coating of purple ink, such as found in an indelible pencil, neutralizes the yellow, producing a whiter-looking stone. This can be easily detected by washing the stone in alcohol or water. If you have any questions about the color, tactfully request that the stone be washed (in front of you) for better examination. A reputable jeweler should have no objection to this request.

Improving the color by using a sputtering technique. This technique (also called "painting" the diamond) involves sputtering a very thin coating of a special substance over the stone or part of the stone, usually the back, where it will be harder to detect when mounted. The girdle area can also be "painted" with the substance and create the same effect. The substance, like indelible pencil, also neutralizes the yellow and thereby improves the color by as much as seven color grades, but unlike indelible ink, *the substance will not wash off.* It can be removed in two ways: by rubbing the stone briskly and firmly with a cleanser, or by boiling the stone carefully in sulfuric acid. If the stone is already mounted and is coated on the back, using cleanser is not feasible. The sulfuric acid method is the only way. *But please note:* using sulfuric acid can be extremely dangerous and must be done only by an experienced person. I cannot overstate the hazards of conducting this test.

This technique is not frequently used, but stones treated in this manner do appear often enough to be worth mentioning.

Coating the diamond with chemicals and baking it in a small lab-type oven. This technique also tends to neutralize some of the yellow, thereby producing a better color grade. This coating will be removed eventually by repeated hot ultrasonic cleanings, which will gradually erode the coating. A more rapid removal can be accomplished by the more dangerous method of boiling in sulfuric acid.

Treated stones must be represented as "treated stones" and should be priced accordingly. Unfortunately, too often, in their passage through many hands, the fact that they have been treated ("radiated" or "bombarded") is overlooked or forgotten—intentionally or accidentally. Whether the color is natural or treated can often be determined by spectroscopic examination, which can be provided by a gem-testing laboratory (see appendix). Not all gemologists, however, are competent with spectroscopic procedures, and some fancy-color diamonds require examination with very sophisticated equipment not available to most labs. If your gemologist lacks the skill or equipment, stones can be submitted to a laboratory such as the GIA's Gem Trade Laboratory for verification.

Most *natural* fancy-color diamonds sold by jewelers in the United States are accompanied by a GIA report.

Erroneous Color Grading

Mistakes in grading of color may be unintentional (resulting from insufficient training or experience, or simply from carelessness), or they may be deliberate. You're safer considering the purchase of a stone that has had such important data as color described in a diamond grading report (or certificate) issued by one of several different laboratories offering this service. Many jewelry firms now offer diamonds accompanied by grading reports; those issued by the GIA are the most widely used in the United States. Diamonds accompanied by reports usually sell for slightly more per carat, but they provide an element of security for the average consumer as well as credible documentation if you wish to sell this stone at some future time. If the stone you are considering is accompanied by such a report, be sure to verify that the information on the certificate is accurate by taking the stone to a competent gemologist or lab.

Clarity Enhancement and Flaw Concealment

Clarity Enhancement

Be especially alert to the possibility that clarity may be enhanced. The two most frequently used techniques are lasering inclusions and filling fractures. In both cases, dark inclusions or cracks that might normally be visible—in some cases, very visible—are concealed or become much less noticeable (these techniques are discussed in chapter 7). Be sure to ask whether or not the stone has been lasered or filled. As long as you know, and pay the right price, a clarity-enhanced diamond may be an attractive choice.

Flaw Concealment

Where possible, flaws are concealed by their settings. A good stone setter will try to set a stone in such a manner that the setting will help to conceal any visible imperfections. For this reason, flaws near or at the girdle will downgrade a stone less than those in the center of a stone; since most settings cover all or part of the girdle, they are simply less visible here. Indeed, a setting can make a flaw "invisible."

There is nothing fraudulent in such uses of settings as long as the stone is properly represented. The only danger is that not only the customer but also the jeweler may not have seen the imperfection concealed by the setting.

Can concealment affect value? In most diamonds other than grade FL or grade IF, the presence of a minor flaw concealed under a prong will not affect the price significantly. However, given the difference in price between diamonds graded FL or IF and VVS_1, a minor blemish or inclusion hidden by the setting that might result in a VVS_1 stone being graded FL could have a significant effect on value, especially if the stone has exceptionally fine color. For this reason, FL or IF stones should be viewed *unmounted*.

Certification of Diamonds

Today, most fine diamonds weighing one carat or more are carefully evaluated by a respected laboratory and are issued a diamond grading report before being set. That report both certifies the diamond as genuine and describes it, providing such important information as color grade, flaw grade, weight, cutting and proportioning, and so on. If you are considering the purchase of a very fine diamond weighing one carat or more and it is *not* accompanied by such a report, I would strongly recommend that you or the seller have the stone evaluated by the GIA or another respected laboratory before purchase. You should do so even if it means having a stone that is already set removed from the setting and reset. Given the significant difference in cost that can result from a grading error in the rarer grades, I believe this procedure is worth the inconvenience and expense.

Unfortunately, the confidence of the public in stones accompanied by certificates has given rise to the practice of altering and counterfeiting them. While you can be relatively sure that "certificated" stones sold by reputable, established jewelry firms are what they claim to be, some suppliers and dealers seize opportunities to prey on the unsuspecting.

Altering Certificates

Sometimes information is changed on an otherwise valid certificate; for example, the flaw or color grade may be altered. If you have any question regarding the information on the certificate, a phone call to the lab, giving them the certificate number and date, will enable you to verify the information on the certificate.

Counterfeit Certificates

Producing a certificate from a nonexistent lab is an increasingly common problem. Stones accompanied by fancy "certificates" from impressive-sounding labs that don't exist are appearing more and more frequently. If the certificate is not from one of the recognized labs (see appendix), it should be carefully checked. Have reputable jewelers in the area heard of this lab? Has the Better Business Bureau had any complaints? If the lab seems legitimate, call to verify the information on the certificate, and if all seems in order, you can probably rest comfortably. Otherwise, you may need to have the facts verified by another gemologist or recognized lab.

Some jewelers may not allow verification of an existing certificate by a little-known lab simply because they've been victims themselves or it isn't worth the inconvenience to them. In this case, you might ask the jeweler to get the stone certificated by one of the recognized labs. Many jewelers today are happy to provide this service. If not, then you must decide how badly you want the stone, how much you feel you can trust the jeweler, and what degree of monetary risk you can afford.

Switching the Stone Described on a Report

In some cases the report is bona fide but the stone has been switched. To protect both the consumer and the lab, some labs are taking advantage of ingenious techniques to ensure against switching. For example, a service called Gemprint uses laser technology to display a diamond's unique pattern of reflection and then records it photographically. The result is an electronic "fingerprint" of the diamond, which can be used for identification purposes (see chapter 18). In addition, the GIA and other labs can now actually inscribe its report number, which is visible only under magnification, directly onto the diamond, along the girdle. By so doing, one can very easily be sure a specific stone matches a specific certificate simply by matching the numbers. There is an additional fee for this service.

In the absence of such a mark, one clue to a switched stone might be provided by comparing the carat weight and dimensions given on the report. If the measurements and weight match exactly, the probability is slim that the stone has been switched, provided the report hasn't been altered. But it's always a good idea to contact the lab to confirm the details of the report, and then double-check all the information. If the measurements don't match, the type and placement of inclusions or blemishes might enable you to determine if the stone in question is the one described on the report but has been altered; the dimensions might differ if, for example, the stone was nicked or chipped and subsequently recut or repolished. In such a case, ask the jeweler to place the stone under the microscope to enable you to see what should be in the stone.

Unfortunately, if the stone has been mounted, it may be difficult to get precise measurements to compare. In this case, if there is any cause for suspicion, you may be taking a risk to buy the stone unless the seller allows you to have the stone removed from the setting and to have both the report and the stone verified by a qualified gemologist-appraiser. This arrangement requires an understanding in writing that the stone can be returned within a certain time limit if the customer learns it is not as represented.

Always make sure in this situation, for both your protection and the jeweler's, that the jeweler writes down on the bill of sale or memo *all* of the stone's dimensions as best as can be determined: diameter or length and width, depth, and weight. This is to help ensure that you aren't accused of switching the stone after leaving the premises in the event you must return it.

Avoid "Bargains"—And Avoid Costly Mistakes

Take time to do your homework first, to learn what to look for and what questions to ask. Keep my recommended four-step procedure in mind, then shop carefully and compare stones being offered by several fine jewelers in your community. This will give you a chance to get a clearer sense of what something should legitimately sell for, decide whether or not something sounds "too good to be true," and, most important, make sounder decisions about which jeweler is asking a *fair* price.

And remember: No one gives away a valuable gem. There are very few "steals," and even fewer people are qualified to truly know a "steal" when they see one.

Is It a Diamond or a Diamond Imposter?

How can you tell if a stone is really a diamond? As I have said many times, unless you are an expert—or consult one—you cannot be sure about the identification of a stone. Nevertheless, there are a few simple tests you can perform that will show up most diamond imposters quite quickly. Here are a few things to look for.

Is newsprint readable or observable through the stone? If the stone is a round, modern-cut stone and is loose or mounted in such a way as to allow you to place it table-down over some small newsprint, check whether you can see or read any portion of the lettering. If so, it is not a diamond. Refraction of light within a genuine diamond will prevent you from being able to see any of the letters in the newsprint.

Is the stone glued into the setting? Diamonds are seldom glued in. Rhinestones often are.

Is the back open or closed? If the stone is a properly set diamond, the back of the setting will usually be open, allowing you to readily see a portion of the pavilion. Some *antique* pieces containing rose-cut or single-cut diamonds may have closed backs, and some of today's finest custom designers may use a closed-back technique. Otherwise, if a piece has a closed back it is probably rhinestone, the back being closed to conceal silver foil applied to the back of the stone to create greater brilliance.

Recently a young woman called and asked if I would examine an antique diamond ring she'd inherited from her great-grandmother. She mentioned that as she was cleaning it, one of its two diamonds had fallen out of the setting, and inside the setting she saw what she described as pieces of "mirror." She added, "Isn't that strange?" Of course my suspicions were immediately aroused, and upon examination of the piece, they were completely confirmed.

When I saw the ring, I could immediately understand why she felt it was a valuable heirloom. It was beautiful, with a classic design. It held two "diamonds" appearing to be approximately one carat each. The ring mounting was finely worked platinum filigree. But the design of the mounting, which had been common in her great-grandmother's day, made viewing the stones from the side of the ring almost impossible. The top of the stone and the beautiful platinum work were visible, but little more. Furthermore, the back was not completely enclosed; a small round hole would easily have led to the assumption that the stones were the real thing, since the setting wasn't completely closed, as were most imitations at that time. The "set" diamond appeared to be a well-proportioned old-mine cut with very good color. The loose stone, however, with some of the "shiny stuff" still clinging to it, lacked brilliance and fire.

This was one of the finest examples of fraud I had seen in a long time. The "stones" were well cut and proportioned; the mounting was beautifully worked in a precious metal; the stones were held by very small prongs, which was typical of good design at that time. But inside the mounting, backing the stones, was silver foil. They were not genuine diamonds but foil-backed glass.

The use of silver foil is an effective method to "create" a diamond. It acts as a mirror to reflect light and makes the stone appear so brilliant and lively that it can pass as a diamond. The foiling seen today consists of making the back facets into true mirrors and then giving the backs of these mirrors a protective coating of gilt paint. These are then set in jewelry so that their backs are hidden.

It's a sad story, but not an altogether uncommon one. I don't know how many more rings as cleverly done exist today, but approximately 5 percent of the antique jewelry we see is set with fake gems. Fine glass imitations (often referred to as "paste") have been with us since the Venetians of the Renaissance period perfected the art of glassmaking. Fraud, unfortunately, has been with us since time immemorial. Don't allow yourself to be deluded into believing that something you possess is "genuine" simply because it is "antique" or has "been in the family" for a long time.

How many facets are visible on the top? In cheaper glass imitations, only nine top facets are usually visible, as opposed to thirty-three visible top facets in a diamond or "good" simulation. Single-cut or Swiss-cut diamonds (see chapter 5) will also show only nine facets on top, but they will be set in open-back mountings, whereas cheap glass imitations are usually set in closed-back mountings.

Does the girdle of the stone appear to be "frosted?" The girdles of most diamonds are unpolished, with a ground-glass–like appearance that suggests frostiness. Some diamond imitations also have a frosted appearance, but of all of these, a diamond has the whitest frostiness—like clean, dry, ground glass. On the other hand, some diamonds do have polished or faceted girdles, and thus no frostiness will be present. You can develop an eye for this by asking a reliable jeweler to point out the differences between a polished girdle, an unpolished girdle, and a faceted girdle.

Is the cut symmetrical? Since diamond is so valuable and symmetry so important to its overall appearance and desirability, the symmetry of the faceting on a diamond will be very carefully executed, whereas in diamond simulations the symmetry of the facets may be sloppy. For example, the eight kite-shaped facets (sometimes called bezel facets) will often be missing one or more points on the side, or on the top or bottom, showing a small straight edge rather than a point. This sloppy faceting can be an important indication that the stone in question is not a diamond, since it indicates that the cutter did not take proper care. It should be noted that some poorer-grade or old-cut diamonds may also show sloppiness.

Are the crown and the pavilion of the stone properly aligned? While occasionally a diamond may show partial misalignment, imitations are frequently and often badly misaligned.

Are the facet edges or faces scratched, chipped, or worn? Diamond imitations include some stones that are very soft and/or brittle, such as zircon, GGG (an artificial simulation), Fabulite (an artificial diamond simulation also known as Wellington Diamond), and glass. Because of their lack of hardness and, in the case of zircon, possible brittleness, these imitations will show wear easily, and one can often detect scratches or chips on the facet edges or faces. The edges are somewhat more vulnerable, and scratches or chips may be more easily seen there, so check the edges first. Then check the flat faces for scratches. Check both the areas that would be most exposed and the areas around the prongs, where a setter might have accidentally scratched the stone while setting it.

Zircon, a stone found in nature that is often confused with cubic zirconia (CZ), an artificial imitation, is relatively hard but very brittle, so it will almost always show chipping at the edges of the facets if the stone has been worn in jewelry for a year or more. Glass and Fabulite will also show scratches after minimal exposure to handling and wear. Fabulite further differs from diamond in its fire; it will show even more fire than diamond, but with a strong bluish cast.

In addition, with a very good eye or the aid of a magnifier, you can examine the lines or edges where the facets come together in these imitation materials. In diamond, these facet edges are very sharp because of the stone's spectacular hardness. In most simulations, however, since the stone is so much softer, the final polishing technique rounds off those edges, and that sharpness is absent.

Some diamond look-alikes, however, are more durable and resistant to noticeable wear. These include colorless synthetic spinel, colorless synthetic sapphire, colorless quartz, YAG (yttrium aluminum garnet; artificial), and CZ. While these may scratch or chip over time with regular wear and daily abuse, scratches or chips are not as numerous and will be less noticeable.

An Important Word about Cubic Zirconia

Cubic zirconia is the best diamond simulation made to date, and even some jewelers have mistaken these stones for diamonds. Shortly after its appearance, several well-known jewelers in Washington, D.C., found themselves stuck with CZ instead of the one-carat diamonds they thought they'd purchased. The crooks were very clever. A well-dressed couple would arrive at the diamond counter and ask to see various one-carat round, brilliant-cut loose diamonds. Because of their fine appearance and educated manner, the jewelers relaxed their guard. The couple would then leave, not making a purchase decision just then, but promising to return. When the jewelers went to replace their merchandise, something didn't seem quite right. Upon close examination, the jewelers discovered that the "nice couple" had pocketed the genuine diamonds and substituted CZ.

Cubic zirconia is almost as brilliant as diamond, has even greater fire (which masks its lesser brilliance), and is relatively hard, giving it good durability and wearability. It is also being produced today in fancy colors—red, green, and yellow—and can provide a nice diamond alternative as a means to offset or dress up colored stones in jewelry if diamonds are unaffordable.

But make sure you *know* what you are buying. For example, if you are shown a lovely amethyst or sapphire ring dressed up with "diamonds," make sure to ask whether the colorless stones are diamonds. And if you are having your own piece of jewelry custom made, you might want to consider using CZ. You can ask your jeweler to order them for you. CZ makes attractive jewelry that can be worn every day without worry.

How Can You Tell If You Have a CZ?

Some of the tests already discussed may help you detect a CZ. The following, however, may eliminate any remaining doubt.

If it is a loose stone, have it weighed. If you are familiar with diamond sizes (see pages 67 and 68) or have a spread gauge (which can be purchased for under $10), you can estimate the diamond carat weight by its spread. A loose stone can be weighed on a scale, which most jewelers have handy, and you can determine how much it should weigh if it is truly a diamond. If the weight is much greater than the diamond weight should be, based on its spread, then it is not a diamond. A CZ is approximately 75 percent heavier than a diamond of the same spread. For example, a CZ that looks like a 1-carat diamond size-wise will weigh 1¾ carats; a CZ that looks like a ¼-carat diamond in terms of size will weigh approximately ⁴⁰⁄₁₀₀ carat.

Look at the girdle. If the girdle is frosted, a subdued whiteness resembling slightly wet or oiled frosted glass will indicate CZ. Unfortunately, looking at girdles to differentiate between the appearance of frosted CZ and frosted diamond girdles requires considerable experience.

Test the stone with a carbide scriber. CZ can be scratched with a fine-point carbide scriber, also available at most jewelry supply houses for under $15. If the scriber is forcibly pushed perpendicularly to any of the facets (the table being the easiest) and then drawn across this flat surface, you will scratch it. You cannot scratch a diamond except with another diamond. But be sensible and considerate. Don't heedlessly scratch merchandise that doesn't belong to you—particularly if the jeweler or seller doesn't represent the stone as a diamond.

Examine the stone, loose or mounted, for fluorescence. Both CZ and diamond fluoresce, but the colors and intensities will be different.

Use an electronic diamond tester. There are pocket-size diamond testers for under $175 that will tell you whether or not you have a diamond. If you follow the instructions, they are easy to use and fairly reliable. Most won't tell you what you have if it's *not* diamond; they will only confirm whether or not it *is* diamond.

If after these tests you have some questions, take the stone to a qualified gemologist with lab facilities for positive identification.

Synthetic Moissanite—A Sparkling Newcomer

A new diamond imitation is being sold today under the name *moissanite*, although it should be called *synthetic moissanite*, since what is being sold in jewelry stores is not natural but created in laboratories. It is silicon carbide, named after Dr. Moissan, the French scientist who discovered it. Advertisements describe it as one of nature's rarest gems, but it does not occur in nature as a gemstone, only as a microscopic inclusion.

It made news upon its introduction because it fooled most electronic diamond testers (those measuring thermal conductivity), indicating "diamond" when tested! Many concluded from this that it was indistinguishable from diamond, but this is far from the case. It has several distinctive characteristics that immediately separate it from diamond. Nevertheless, synthetic moissanite is being misrepresented as diamond in new and antique jewelry, and there have been several cases in which jewelers have switched stones substituting synthetic moissanite for the original diamond. Gemologists can quickly and easily separate diamond from synthetic moissanite with simple tests, in most cases using only a 10x loupe. There is also new diamond testing equipment that can instantly distinguish between the two.

Synthetic moissanite is lighter than diamond, so weighing it is a quick way to distinguish it from diamond if the stone is unmounted. While moissanite is not as hard as diamond, it is harder than CZ and even harder than ruby and sapphire, which means it is a very durable material that can take a very high polish. It has even greater brilliance and much more dispersion (fire) than either diamond or CZ. One disadvantage in comparison with CZ is that it is much more expensive, costing approximately a tenth of what a comparable diamond costs.

Synthetic moissanite has a distinctive appearance and may make an attractive choice for those who want something new and different. As a diamond imitation, given its high cost and the fact that CZ actually looks more like diamond, only time will tell whether or not it will replace CZ as the diamond imitation of the twenty-first century.

A Word about Synthetic Diamonds

Synthetic diamonds are diamonds that are made in the laboratory. Unlike CZ, moissanite, and other diamond imitations, all of which differ from diamond physically and chemically, synthetic diamond *duplicates* the natural. That is, it is scientifically produced in a laboratory with virtually the same physical and chemical properties. In essence, it is diamond. But it is not identical. Since it is grown in laboratories, it shows distinctive growth features not seen in natural diamonds, so all synthetic diamonds now being produced can be distinguished from natural diamonds. In many cases, however, identification requires sophisticated scientific instrumentation found only in major gem-testing laboratories. For this reason, I once again stress the importance of having laboratory documentation for any fine diamond. *Note:* Electronic diamond testers have become very popular and are very effective in distinguishing diamond imitations, such as CZ, YAG, Fabulite, and others, from diamond. However, they cannot distinguish between synthetic and natural diamonds, and they *will* indicate "diamond" when testing synthetic diamond.

Synthetic gem-quality diamonds are now commercially available in a range of sizes, shapes, and colors. Yellow, blue, pink, and red stones are now being produced in sizes up to two carats and are creating a sensation in the marketplace because they provide very beautiful alternatives to their much rarer, and much costlier, natural counterparts. Deep green synthetic diamonds may also be available soon. Where colorless and near-colorless synthetic diamonds are concerned, laboratories have succeeded in producing them, but production costs are still too high for them to be commercially viable at this time.

Comparison of Diamonds and Diamond Look-Alikes

Name of Stone	Hardness (Mohs' Scale 1–10) 1 = Soft, 10 = Hardest	Read-through*	Degree of Dispersion (Fire, Flashes of Color Observed)	Wearability
Diamond	10 (Hardest natural substance in existence)	None, if properly cut	High; lots of fire and liveliness	Excellent
Strontium titanate (also known as Fabulite or Wellington Diamond)	5–6 (Soft)	None, if properly cut	Extremely high; too high (much more than diamond); shows lots of blue flashes	Poor—scratches and wears badly
Cubic zirconia (CZ)	8.5 (Hard)	Slight	Very high; lots of life	Very good
Gadolinium gallium garnet (GGG; produced very briefly)	6.5 (Somewhat soft)	Moderate	High; almost identical to diamond	Fair—scratches easily; wears badly; sunlight causes brownish discoloration
Yttrium aluminum garnet (YAG; used extensively)	8.5 (Hard)	Strong	Very low; almost no visible display of fire	Good
Synthetic rutile (shows yellowish color)	6.5 (Soft)	None	Extremely high; lots of life—but strong yellowish flashes	Poor; scratches easily and shows excessive wear
Zircon	7.5 (Moderately hard)	Moderate	Good; lively	Fair—hard but brittle, so chips easily and shows wear equivalent to much softer stones
Synthetic sapphire	9 (Very hard)	Very strong	Very low; little life or display of color flashes	Very good
Synthetic spinel	8 (Hard)	Very strong	Low; little "life"	Very good
Glass	5–6.5 (Soft)	Very strong	Variable—low to good depending on quality of glass and cut	Poor; susceptible to scratches, chipping, and excessive wear
Synthetic moissanite	9.25 (Very hard)	None	Extremely high; much too high for diamond; higher than CZ	Excellent

*This technique—the ability and ease with which one can read print while looking through the stone—is reliable only when looking at round, brilliant-cut stones (although it is *sometimes* useful for ovals and some fancy cuts).

CHAPTER ELEVEN

Comparing Diamond Prices

A ll too often, people look for easy answers to complex problems.
Many would like to have a simple list of diamond grades and corresponding prices, by size. Unfortunately, market conditions are constantly changing, and, more important, significant differences in price
often result from subtle differences in quality not readily discernible to
any but the professional. Therefore, it is not possible to provide a simple
answer to this complex question.

But that does not mean I cannot provide you with some general
guidelines that will help you understand the *relative* effects of each of
the four primary factors used to determine the value of diamonds. The
following charts are not intended as hard price lists of what you should
be paying in a jewelry store; instead, they should be used as a guide-
line—a foundation on which you can place more current information that
reflects the variations in a constantly fluctuating market. Keep in mind
that these prices are for unmounted stones. Fine settings and custom
designed one-of-a-kind pieces can add substantially to the price.

Extreme differences between the prices given on the following pages
and a price you might be quoted for a diamond should be examined carefully; if the price is *much lower,* be sure to seek a gemologist or gemologist-
appraiser to check the quality and verify that the stone is as represented.
If the price is *much higher,* do some comparison shopping in your community to be sure the seller is offering good value.

Note that the prices given here are for round, brilliant-cut diamonds
with good proportioning; stones with excellent proportioning will sell for
more, while stones with poor proportioning can sell for much less. Diamonds having fancy shapes—shapes other than round—normally sell
for anywhere from 5 to 15 percent less. However, if a particular shape is
in great demand, the price can be higher than for round stones.

Finally, before relying too heavily on the prices listed in this chapter, be sure you read the information on diamond grading reports. This knowledge will give you additional input on adjusting diamond prices according to the more subtle factors that affect quality and value. Finally, if you are contemplating the purchase of a particular stone, be sure to have the facts verified by a qualified gemologist-appraiser.

Retail Price Guide for Round Brilliant-Cut Diamonds*

Notice both the tremendous price fluctuation among stones of the same size due to differences in the flaw grades and color grades, and the disproportionate jumps in cost *per carat*, depending upon size.

lightface indicates PRICE PER CARAT   in U.S. Dollars
boldface indicates PRICE PER STONE

3/4 Carat   COLOR GRADE

FLAW (CLARITY) GRADE

		D	E	F	G	H	I	J	K
IF**		15,200	12,200	11,600	10,600	8,400	7,600	7,200	6,800
		11,400	**9,150**	**8,700**	**7,950**	**6,300**	**5,700**	**5,400**	**5,100**
VVS$_1$		12,400	11,600	10,200	9,000	8,000	7,200	6,800	6,500
		9,300	**8,700**	**7,650**	**6,750**	**6,000**	**5,400**	**5,100**	**4,875**
VVS$_2$		11,200	10,200	9,200	8,200	7,600	7,000	6,700	6,250
		8,400	**7,650**	**6,900**	**6,150**	**5,700**	**5,250**	**5,025**	**4,688**
VS$_1$		9,800	9,000	8,200	7,600	7,300	6,600	6,500	6,000
		7,350	**6,750**	**6,150**	**5,700**	**5,475**	**4,950**	**4,875**	**4,500**
VS$_2$		8,600	8,200	7,800	7,200	6,900	6,500	6,400	5,750
		6,450	**6,150**	**5,850**	**5,400**	**5,175**	**4,875**	**4,800**	**4,313**
SI$_1$		7,600	7,400	7,000	6,800	6,600	6,400	6,250	5,500
		5,700	**5,550**	**5,250**	**5,100**	**4,950**	**4,800**	**4,688**	**4,125**
SI$_2$		6,800	6,500	6,250	6,000	5,900	5,700	5,400	5,000
		5,100	**4,875**	**4,688**	**4,500**	**4,425**	**4,275**	**4,050**	**3,750**
I$_1$		5,500	5,250	5,000	4,750	4,625	4,500	4,250	3,500
		4,125	**3,938**	**3,750**	**3,563**	**3,469**	**3,375**	**3,188**	**2,625**

*   Prices compiled from *The Guide*, Gemworld International, Inc., and adjusted to retail.
**   There is a minimal price difference between FL and IF stones in the rarest colors. Stones will cost approximately 5–8 percent more in D–F colors; 1–2 percent more in G–J colors; there is no cost difference in stones of less rare colors (below J).

Light Carat

FLAW (CLARITY) GRADE

	D	E	F	G	H	I	J	K
IF**	17,400	13,400	12,200	10,800	9,600	8,400	7,600	7,400
	15,660	12,060	10,980	9,720	8,640	7,560	6,840	6,660
VVS₁	13,400	12,200	11,200	9,800	9,000	8,000	7,400	7,000
	12,060	10,980	10,080	8,820	8,100	7,200	6,660	6,300
VVS₂	12,200	11,400	10,200	9,200	8,600	7,800	6,900	6,750
	10,980	10,260	9,180	8,280	7,740	7,020	6,210	6,075
VS₁	11,200	10,000	9,400	9,000	8,400	7,600	6,700	6,500
	10,080	9,000	8,460	8,100	7,560	6,840	6,030	5,850
VS₂	9,800	9,200	8,800	8,400	7,800	7,400	6,400	6,250
	8,820	8,280	7,920	7,560	7,020	6,660	5,760	5,625
SI₁	9,000	8,600	8,200	7,800	7,200	7,000	6,200	6,000
	8,100	7,740	7,380	7,020	6,480	6,300	5,580	5,400
SI₂	8,200	7,800	7,400	7,000	6,000	6,500	6,100	5,500
	7,380	7,020	6,660	6,300	5,400	5,850	5,490	4,950
I₁	6,500	6,250	6,000	5,750	5,500	5,000	4,500	4,000
	5,850	5,625	5,400	5,175	4,950	4,500	4,050	3,600

1 Carat

FLAW (CLARITY) GRADE

	D	E	F	G	H	I	J	K
IF**	28,000	19,200	17,200	13,800	12,200	10,600	9,200	8,200
	28,000	19,200	17,200	13,800	12,200	10,600	9,200	8,200
VVS₁	19,200	17,200	14,800	13,000	11,600	10,000	9,000	7,800
	19,200	17,200	14,800	13,000	11,600	10,000	9,000	7,800
VVS₂	17,000	14,200	13,000	12,200	11,200	9,600	8,800	7,600
	17,000	14,200	13,000	12,200	11,200	9,600	8,800	7,600
VS₁	14,200	13,600	12,800	11,800	11,000	9,200	8,400	7,400
	14,200	13,600	12,800	11,800	11,000	9,200	8,400	7,400
VS₂	12,800	12,200	12,000	11,200	10,400	8,800	7,800	7,000
	12,800	12,200	12,000	11,200	10,400	8,800	7,800	7,000
SI₁	11,400	10,800	10,600	10,000	9,400	8,200	7,400	6,400
	11,400	10,800	10,600	10,000	9,400	8,200	7,400	6,400
SI₂	10,200	9,800	9,400	8,800	8,200	7,200	6,600	6,200
	10,200	9,800	9,400	8,800	8,200	7,200	6,600	6,200
I₁	6,800	6,400	6,200	6,000	5,800	5,400	5,175	4,725
	6,800	6,400	6,200	6,000	5,800	5,400	5,175	4,725

* Prices compiled from *The Guide*, Gemworld International, Inc., and adjusted to retail.
** There is a minimal price difference between FL and IF stones in the rarest colors. Stones will cost approximately 5–8 percent more in D–F colors; 1–2 percent more in G–J colors; there is no cost difference in stones of less rare colors (below J).

2 Carat COLOR GRADE

<table>
<tr><th></th><th>D</th><th>E</th><th>F</th><th>G</th><th>H</th><th>I</th><th>J</th><th>K</th></tr>
<tr><td rowspan="2">IF**</td><td>44,400</td><td>33,400</td><td>29,200</td><td>23,200</td><td>20,200</td><td>15,400</td><td>13,000</td><td>11,000</td></tr>
<tr><td>88,800</td><td>66,800</td><td>58,400</td><td>46,400</td><td>40,400</td><td>30,800</td><td>26,000</td><td>22,000</td></tr>
<tr><td rowspan="2">VVS₁</td><td>32,800</td><td>29,200</td><td>23,600</td><td>21,200</td><td>17,600</td><td>14,800</td><td>12,600</td><td>10,400</td></tr>
<tr><td>65,600</td><td>58,400</td><td>47,200</td><td>42,400</td><td>35,200</td><td>29,600</td><td>25,200</td><td>20,800</td></tr>
<tr><td rowspan="2">VVS₂</td><td>29,200</td><td>24,000</td><td>21,600</td><td>19,200</td><td>16,400</td><td>14,200</td><td>12,200</td><td>10,000</td></tr>
<tr><td>58,400</td><td>48,000</td><td>43,200</td><td>38,400</td><td>32,800</td><td>28,400</td><td>24,400</td><td>20,000</td></tr>
<tr><td rowspan="2">VS₁</td><td>24,600</td><td>22,000</td><td>19,400</td><td>18,400</td><td>15,800</td><td>14,000</td><td>11,400</td><td>9,400</td></tr>
<tr><td>49,200</td><td>44,000</td><td>38,800</td><td>36,800</td><td>31,600</td><td>28,000</td><td>22,800</td><td>18,800</td></tr>
<tr><td rowspan="2">VS₂</td><td>19,200</td><td>19,000</td><td>18,000</td><td>17,400</td><td>14,600</td><td>13,000</td><td>10,400</td><td>8,800</td></tr>
<tr><td>38,400</td><td>38,000</td><td>36,000</td><td>34,800</td><td>29,200</td><td>26,000</td><td>20,800</td><td>17,600</td></tr>
<tr><td rowspan="2">SI₁</td><td>16,600</td><td>16,200</td><td>15,400</td><td>14,800</td><td>13,400</td><td>11,800</td><td>9,600</td><td>8,200</td></tr>
<tr><td>33,200</td><td>32,400</td><td>30,800</td><td>29,600</td><td>26,800</td><td>23,600</td><td>19,200</td><td>16,400</td></tr>
<tr><td rowspan="2">SI₂</td><td>13,200</td><td>13,000</td><td>12,800</td><td>12,000</td><td>11,000</td><td>9,400</td><td>8,600</td><td>7,400</td></tr>
<tr><td>26,400</td><td>26,000</td><td>25,600</td><td>24,000</td><td>22,000</td><td>18,800</td><td>17,200</td><td>14,800</td></tr>
<tr><td rowspan="2">I₁</td><td>7,800</td><td>7,400</td><td>7,200</td><td>7,000</td><td>6,800</td><td>6,600</td><td>6,200</td><td>6,000</td></tr>
<tr><td>15,600</td><td>14,800</td><td>14,400</td><td>14,000</td><td>13,600</td><td>13,200</td><td>12,400</td><td>12,000</td></tr>
</table>

FLAW (CLARITY) GRADE

3 Carat COLOR GRADE

<table>
<tr><th></th><th>D</th><th>E</th><th>F</th><th>G</th><th>H</th><th>I</th><th>J</th><th>K</th></tr>
<tr><td rowspan="2">IF**</td><td>67,600</td><td>47,800</td><td>40,800</td><td>31,400</td><td>25,000</td><td>19,800</td><td>15,400</td><td>14,000</td></tr>
<tr><td>202,800</td><td>143,400</td><td>122,400</td><td>94,200</td><td>75,000</td><td>59,400</td><td>46,200</td><td>42,000</td></tr>
<tr><td rowspan="2">VVS₁</td><td>48,000</td><td>41,000</td><td>31,800</td><td>25,800</td><td>22,400</td><td>17,800</td><td>14,600</td><td>13,400</td></tr>
<tr><td>144,000</td><td>123,000</td><td>95,400</td><td>77,400</td><td>67,200</td><td>53,400</td><td>43,800</td><td>40,200</td></tr>
<tr><td rowspan="2">VVS₂</td><td>41,400</td><td>31,800</td><td>26,600</td><td>23,200</td><td>20,600</td><td>17,000</td><td>14,000</td><td>12,400</td></tr>
<tr><td>124,200</td><td>95,400</td><td>79,800</td><td>69,600</td><td>61,800</td><td>51,000</td><td>42,000</td><td>37,200</td></tr>
<tr><td rowspan="2">VS₁</td><td>32,200</td><td>26,800</td><td>23,600</td><td>22,200</td><td>19,000</td><td>15,600</td><td>12,800</td><td>11,600</td></tr>
<tr><td>96,600</td><td>80,400</td><td>70,800</td><td>66,600</td><td>57,000</td><td>46,800</td><td>38,400</td><td>34,800</td></tr>
<tr><td rowspan="2">VS₂</td><td>26,400</td><td>23,800</td><td>22,400</td><td>19,800</td><td>17,000</td><td>13,800</td><td>11,600</td><td>10,400</td></tr>
<tr><td>79,200</td><td>71,400</td><td>67,200</td><td>59,400</td><td>51,000</td><td>41,400</td><td>34,800</td><td>31,200</td></tr>
<tr><td rowspan="2">SI₁</td><td>21,200</td><td>20,200</td><td>18,800</td><td>17,000</td><td>14,200</td><td>12,400</td><td>10,800</td><td>9,600</td></tr>
<tr><td>63,600</td><td>60,600</td><td>56,400</td><td>51,000</td><td>42,600</td><td>37,200</td><td>32,400</td><td>28,800</td></tr>
<tr><td rowspan="2">SI₂</td><td>16,200</td><td>15,200</td><td>14,200</td><td>13,400</td><td>12,600</td><td>11,200</td><td>9,800</td><td>8,400</td></tr>
<tr><td>48,600</td><td>45,600</td><td>42,600</td><td>40,200</td><td>37,800</td><td>33,600</td><td>29,400</td><td>25,200</td></tr>
<tr><td rowspan="2">I₁</td><td>11,800</td><td>11,000</td><td>10,200</td><td>9,600</td><td>9,000</td><td>8,000</td><td>7,600</td><td>6,800</td></tr>
<tr><td>35,400</td><td>33,000</td><td>30,600</td><td>28,800</td><td>27,000</td><td>24,000</td><td>22,800</td><td>20,400</td></tr>
</table>

FLAW (CLARITY) GRADE

* Prices compiled from *The Guide*, Gemworld International, Inc., and adjusted to retail.
** There is a minimal price difference between FL and IF stones in the rarest colors. Stones will cost approximately 5–8 percent more in D–F colors; 1–2 percent more in G–J colors; there is no cost difference in stones of less rare colors (below J).

CHAPTER TWELVE

Fancy-Color Diamonds

Natural-Color Diamonds— A Rainbow of Choices

Of all the gems on earth, nothing surpasses the palette of natural-color diamonds for beauty, distinctiveness, and desirability. Known as *fancy-color diamonds,* they occur in virtually every color and shade of color. Ruby red, baby pink, grass green, and sapphire blue diamonds rank among the rarest and most precious of all gems.

Fancy-color diamonds possess a distinctive look not found in any other colored gem. Whatever the actual "body" color seen in a fancy-color diamond, it is augmented by the presence of numerous pinpoint flashes of other colors that are the result of diamond's high dispersion—diamond's ability to break up each ray of reflected light into an array of spectral colors. For example, a "yellow" diamond may be yellow, but you may also see pinpoint reflections of green, blue, orange, and so on. The body color of the diamond, combined with its high dispersion, creates a fiery scintillation not found in any other gemstone. Even *brown* diamonds, once regarded as "too common" to use in fine jewelry, are very much in vogue today. Their warm neutral colors and fiery dispersion create a special allure, and since they are so much more affordable than other diamond choices, jewelers worldwide are now showcasing jewelry containing brown diamonds in every shade, from the palest beige to the deepest, richest brown tones.

What Causes the Color Seen in Fancy Diamonds?

When we talk about fancy-color diamonds, we must remember that the color seen can be *natural* or the result of some *treatment* used to transform an off-color diamond into a lovely "fancy" color.

Natural color in diamonds usually results from the presence of trace elements, although in some cases it can result from natural exposure to radiation (as the diamond was forming in the earth), or from damage to the crystal lattice structure. Natural-color yellow diamonds get their color from the presence of nitrogen, for example, and blue diamonds, from boron or hydrogen. In diamonds where color is due to particular trace elements, the presence or absence of those trace elements can be ascertained through sophisticated testing procedures, providing an important key to determining whether color is natural or artificial.

The situation is different with green diamonds. The color seen in natural-color green diamonds does not result from the presence of trace elements; green diamonds owe their color to exposure to radiation as they were forming in the earth, eons ago. This creates an unusual dilemma for gem-testing laboratories because there are also treated green diamonds that have been created by humans using modern radiation techniques. Since radiation is the cause of color in both cases, it poses some identification challenges for laboratories. In some cases a natural-color green diamond will contain certain unique identifying characteristics that distinguish it from the treated stone, and in some cases a treated green diamond will exhibit characteristics that identify it as treated, but many green diamonds lack conclusive evidence for positive identification. In such cases, a laboratory report will indicate that a positive determination cannot be made with gemological data currently available. This leaves the door open to the possibility that a positive determination might be made at some future time as new data comes to light from continued research and technological advances, but there are no guarantees. In any event, if you are considering a natural green diamond you must understand that it may be more difficult to find one with laboratory documentation confirming that the color is natural.

Fortunately, gem-testing laboratories are usually able to positively confirm origin of color in fancy-color diamonds, and cases where they cannot are the exception rather than the rule. For this reason, and since origin of color has such a significant impact on rarity and cost, I never recommend the purchase of a natural-color diamond without laboratory verification (see appendix) nor would I ever purchase one personally without such documentation.

Judging Fancy-Color Diamonds

Fancy-color diamonds have always attracted connoisseurs and collectors, but today they are capturing the attention of a much wider audience. Demand—and pricing—are setting new records. If a fancy-color diamond is what you seek, take time to learn as much as you can about the specific colors you like and what is available; some colors occur in a wider range of sizes than others, and some are much rarer. And most of all, before buying, no matter how rare the color, no matter how collectible or desirable to others, make sure you *like* it!

It is also important to take time to understand the four Cs as they relate to fancy-color diamonds—especially the subtle nuances of color and their impact on value—and to develop an eye for the important differences that affect not only the beauty and desirability of a particular stone, but its cost. And finally, since most natural-color diamonds are accompanied by a diamond report, be sure to take time to understand what the information provided on the report is really telling you.

Let's begin with the most important factor you must judge: color.

Color—The Most Important Factor

While the four Cs apply to fancy-color diamonds as well as to colorless diamonds, the emphasis is clearly on "color." In general, the rarer the color, the less impact clarity and cutting have on its value; the less rare the color, the more important clarity and cutting become. Many reports on fancy-color diamonds do not even include a clarity grade or information regarding cutting and proportioning except for the stone's shape.

When judging a fancy-color diamond, color is so paramount that it is important to understand how color is graded. You must carefully evaluate each of the following:

- Purity of color
- Depth of color (tone and saturation)
- Color distribution throughout the stone

Whether or not the color is *natural*—the origin of color—is also critically important, as I've already discussed, in the overall evaluation of color and its impact on price.

To properly evaluate the color of a fancy-color diamond, the stone must be viewed from the *face-up* position—looking at it with the table up, as you would see it when mounted in a piece of jewelry—which is very different from evaluating colorless diamonds (see chapter 6). From the face-up position, you must now evaluate each of the following characteristics:

Purity of color. This refers to the hue and the purity of the hue. Let's take "yellow" as an example. The color of a fancy yellow diamond might be described as "yellow," "orangish yellow," "brownish yellow," "brown yellow," and so on. Understanding the differences in the wording is very important. The final word in the color description is the *hue;* the word or words preceding it are the *modifiers* of the hue. Having no modifier means the color is a pure hue, which, depending upon the color, can be very rare. Some color combinations are rarer and costlier than others. For example, let's consider two diamonds where one is "orangy yellow" and the other is "brownish yellow." In both cases, the hue is "yellow" but since orange is rarer than brown, the orangy yellow stone would be more valuable than the brownish yellow stone.

Now let's look again at the description of the "brownish yellow" stone. Here the primary color is yellow, with a lesser degree of brown modifying the color. However, if the words were *reversed*—that is, yellowish *brown* rather than brownish *yellow*—the words would tell us the diamond is *brown* with some lesser amount of yellow modifying the color. Again, since brown is a much less rare color, a yellowish brown diamond would have less value than a brownish yellow.

When considering a fancy-color diamond it is important to take time to understand the terminology used to describe the particular hue that interests you, what shades are available, and how they compare in terms of rarity and value.

Depth of color. This refers to the *saturation* of color combined with the *tone.* Saturation refers to the denseness of the color. A pure yellow or pink diamond, for example, has minimal color saturation, while a brown or blue diamond has heavy color saturation. Most fancy-color diamonds occur in less saturated colors such as yellow. With the exception of brown diamonds, heavily saturated colors can be very rare and costly; ruby red and sapphire blue are among the rarest and costliest of all gems.

Tone has to do with how much *white* or *black* is present; that is, how "light" or "dark" the color is. If there is too much white, it will be too pale or even colorless; if there is too much black, the stone will be overly dark. Fancy "black" diamonds are popular today. These are typically opaque (that is, not transparent) and heavily included and usually sell for much less than other fancy colors. It is important to note that today black diamonds are being used increasingly in designer lines, but most of the stones used are being treated to obtain the black color. There are also "white" diamonds that should not be confused with "colorless" stones. Fancy white diamonds are very rare, but they are usually milky or cloudy, which reduces their popularity and value.

Most diamond reports for fancy-color diamonds classify the depth of color using terminology similar to the following:

- *Faint*
- *Very Light*
- *Light*
  (these first three categories are not truly "fancy colors")
- *Fancy Light*
- *Fancy (Yellow, Orange, Brown, Blue, or whatever the color)*
- *Fancy Dark*
- *Fancy Deep*
- *Fancy Intense*
- *Fancy Vivid*

The classification pertaining to the depth of color is extremely important. One tonal difference can dramatically affect value. But it is important to understand that the *number of classifications* is *not the same for every color.* Generally speaking, less saturated colors (such as pure yellow or pure pink) have fewer classifications, and more heavily saturated colors (such as blue) will have more classifications. If you are interested in a yellow diamond, for example, and decide you want a color that is richer than "Fancy Yellow," the next classification following "Fancy Yellow" is usually "Intense" rather than "Dark" or "Deep," although in some rare cases you will find a "Deep" classification. On the other hand, if you are looking at a diamond described as "Fancy *Brownish* Yellow"—which has a higher color saturation—you will find more tonal classifications, and it is not unusual to find a "Fancy Deep" classification that would have more color depth than "Fancy" but less than "Intense." It would also be more expensive than "Fancy Brownish Yellow" but less expensive than "Fancy

Intense." In blue diamonds, you can also find a "Dark" and a "Deep" classification. And so on. What this really means is that *to accurately evaluate rarity and value, and to be sure you have found the depth of color that best suits your needs, you must be sure to find out what the specific tonal classifications are for the particular color you are considering.*

Evenness of color. A laboratory report will indicate whether or not the color is evenly dispersed under "Distribution." Ideally, the distribution of the color should be "even," but this is not always the case. Sometimes color occurs in zones, alternating with colorless zones, and the report will indicate "uneven" color distribution. Such stones may *appear* to have even color distribution when viewed from the top, and may be lovely and desirable, but they should cost less than one that has "even" distribution.

Is the Color Natural?

In addition to the rainbow of colors in which diamond occurs naturally, diamonds can also be transformed into beautiful, desirable colors by several techniques, as mentioned earlier. Radiation techniques have been used for many years to change tinted, off-white diamonds into various shades of yellow, green, and blue-green. In most cases (green diamonds are often an exception), these can be easily distinguished from the natural by any competent gemologist. But new techniques are creating new challenges, and determining whether or not color is natural may require very sophisticated, high-tech procedures only available at a major gem-testing laboratory.

HPHT process creates "fancy-color" diamonds. Earlier I mentioned a new technique known as *high-pressure/high-temperature annealing* (HPHT) that can be used to transform very off-white and brownish diamonds into colorless and near-colorless diamonds (see page 46). HPHT techniques can also transform tinted off-white and brownish diamonds into a variety of "fancy" colors, from yellowish green and greenish yellow to exquisite shades of pink and blue. While the yellowish green and greenish yellow stones often have a distinctive look that sets them apart from most natural diamonds of comparable color, this is not the case with the pink and blue stones, which exhibit a color and other characteristics that make it very difficult to distinguish them from the natural.

Since natural fancy-color diamonds can be costlier than many colorless diamonds—and fancy-color blue and pink diamonds *much* costlier because of their rarity—I recommend that you obtain a laboratory report for any fancy-color diamond represented to have natural color. Most major labs will grade diamonds treated in this manner, indicating the treatment in a special comment on the report (see sample fancy diamond reports at the end of this chapter).

There is nothing wrong with buying a diamond that has obtained its color through some form of treatment. Increasingly, fine jewelry designers are using color-treated diamonds to create very distinctive jewelry, at attractive prices. But it is important to know whether the color is natural or the result of some treatment process so that you know you have paid an appropriate price.

An extra word of caution regarding pink and blue diamonds: Anyone considering the purchase of a diamond represented to be *natural blue* or *natural pink* must be sure it is accompanied by a *current* report—*a report issued by a major laboratory after December 2000.* If the date on the report is earlier than December 2000, request that the stone be resubmitted to a major lab for verification, or make the sale contingent upon getting this documentation (see appendix). Most laboratories were unaware of the use of HPHT techniques to create blue and pink colors until the year 2000, and diagnostic data with which to detect the treatment was not available until later that year. Since prior testing techniques would not have revealed the treatment, earlier reports may not be accurate.

Clarity

Many fancy-color diamond reports do not include a clarity grade, especially if the color is exceptional or very rare. When a clarity grade is provided, the grading is based on the same criteria used for colorless diamonds (see chapter 7). It is important to understand that in fancy-color diamonds, flawlessness is even rarer than in colorless diamonds. Fancy-color diamonds are often graded "slightly imperfect" (SI), and "imperfect" (I) grades are also common. In fancy-color stones, SI and I grades do not carry the stigma associated with these grades in colorless diamonds, especially if the stone has a rare or unusually deep color. This is not to say that there are no "flawless" fancy-color diamonds, or stones in the rarer clarity grades, but if the color is rare, and the stone also has a rarer clarity grade, the cost will be disproportionately *much* higher.

As with colorless diamonds, enhancement techniques are also being used to improve the appearance by filling fractures and lasering black inclusions so they will no longer be visible. Be sure to take the precautions recommended in chapter 7.

Cutting and Proportioning

As already mentioned, most reports on fancy-color diamonds lack information pertaining to cutting and proportioning. As with clarity, the deeper and/or rarer the color, the less important the cutting. However, I should mention here that certain shapes are more common among fancy-color diamonds because, in addition to its proportioning, the shape itself and the cutting style (that is, step cut versus brilliant cut) can affect the intensity or evenness of the color.

Shape Can Affect Intensity and Evenness of Color

If you are interested in a fancy-color diamond, you must allow some flexibility where shape is concerned. Certain shapes are rare and difficult, if not impossible, to find in fancy colors, while other shapes are much more readily available, in almost any color. The emerald cut is one that is especially difficult to find, and even round stones may be difficult to find in a particular color. The radiant cut, however, is frequently found.

Today's modern radiant and princess cuts have become especially popular for fancy-color diamonds, because the shape, proportioning, and facet arrangement result in *intensifying the color*. On the other hand, it is extremely rare to find a fancy-color diamond in an emerald cut, because the color won't look as intense. In fact, when emerald-cut diamonds with fancy colors are found in old jewelry, many diamond cutters immediately recut them into one of the new cuts, such as the radiant or princess, to intensify the color so they can obtain a report with a rarer color grade. I searched for an emerald-cut diamond with an "Intense Yellow" color for a client and it took many months to find just three stones, because "Intense Yellow" emerald-cut diamonds, recut and resubmitted to a laboratory, often receive a "*Vivid*" grade, the rarest and costliest of yellow diamonds.

The result is that emerald-cut diamonds in fancy colors are becoming ever more difficult to find. One of the most beautiful diamonds I ever saw was a square emerald-cut diamond, with a report that graded the color "Vivid Yellow." Imagine an emerald cut with a "Vivid" grade, and the intensity of color! The stone's personality was truly regal, and I would certainly never want to see this stone recut because I appreciate its rarity—not just because its color is "Vivid" but because it is a "Vivid" emerald cut.

Some shapes are not desirable in a fancy-color diamond because they may cause the color to appear uneven. This is often the case when a fancy-color diamond is cut into a pear shape or marquise shape. This is because these shapes usually exhibit a *bow tie* effect across the center of the stone—an effect created by light leakage—which usually causes the color to appear lighter across the area of the bow tie. Sometimes the difference is slight, sometimes it is pronounced. Such stones should sell for less; the more visible the color difference, the more impact on cost.

Now that you have a better understanding of how fancy-color diamonds are judged, you're ready to start searching for that special stone. It may seem somewhat complicated at first, but if you focus on the factors discussed here, it won't be long before you discover what is important to you and what you really like; it will quickly become a fascinating and exciting journey, filled with wonder and joy.

To help you become more familiar with fancy-color diamond reports and the types of documentation that you might encounter, the following pages provide sample reports from some of the world's most respected laboratories. Following the reports are price guides for fancy-color diamonds, fancy-color diamonds sold at auction, and fancy-color synthetic diamonds. Since some fancy-color diamonds are so rare, the auction arena often provides the best indication of current value. In the guide below are some examples of what some fancy-color diamonds have brought at auction.

New York Headquarters
580 Fifth Avenue | New York, NY 10036-4794
T: 212-221-5858 | F: 212-575-3095

Carlsbad
5355 Armada Drive | Carlsbad, CA 92008-4699
T: 760-603-4500 | F: 760-603-1814

COLORED DIAMOND
GRADING REPORT

112565702

GIA REPORT 10958099

January 03, 2000

Laser Inscription Registry .... GIA 10958099

Shape and Cutting Style .... CUT-CORNERED
RECTANGULAR MODIFIED BRILLIANT

Measurements .... 6.59 x 5.99 x 3.75 mm

Weight .... 1.18 carat

Proportions

Depth .... 62.6 %

Table .... 63 %

Girdle .... MEDIUM TO SLIGHTLY THICK

Culet .... VERY SMALL

Finish

Polish .... VERY GOOD

Symmetry .... VERY GOOD

Clarity Grade VS1

Color

Origin .... NATURAL

Grade .... FANCY
YELLOW

Distribution .... EVEN

Fluorescence .... NONE

Comments:
Sample Sample Sample Sample Sample Sample

Additional Inscription .... FOREVER YOURS, JOHN

GIA
CLARITY
SCALE

GIA
COLORED
DIAMOND
SCALE

FLAWLESS

INTERNALLY
FLAWLESS

VVS₁

VVS₂

VS₁

VS₂

SI₁

SI₂

I₁

I₂

I₃

This Report is not a guarantee, valuation or appraisal. This Report contains only the characteristics of the diamond described herein after it has been graded, tested, examined and analyzed by GIA Gem Trade Laboratory under 10X magnification, and/or has been inscribed, using the techniques and equipment available to GIA Gem Trade Laboratory at the time of the examination and/or at the time of being inscribed, including fully corrected triplet loupe and binocular microscope, master color comparison diamonds, standardized viewing environment and light source, electronic carat balance, high intensity short wave fluorescence imaging system, optical measuring device, micro laser inscribing device, ProportionScope®, ultraviolet lamps, millimeter gauge, additional visual color comparators, spectroscope, Illuminator Polariscope®, immersion liquids, ultraviolet-visible and infrared spectrometers, X-ray fluorescence spectrometer, gamma-ray spectroscopy systems, beta radiation scintillation detector, radiation survey meter, X-ray luminescence equipment, and ancillary instruments as necessary. Red symbols denote internal characteristics (inclusions). Green or black symbols denote external characteristics (blemishes). Diagram is an approximate representation of the diamond, and symbols shown indicate type, position, and approximate size of clarity characteristics. All clarity characteristics may not be shown. Details of finish are not shown. The recipient of this Report may wish to consult a credentialed Jeweler or Gemologist about the importance and interrelationship of cut, color, clarity and carat weight.

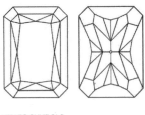

KEY TO SYMBOLS
° Crystal
⌐ Feather
Natural

Here you will find information indicating origin of color ("natural"), depth of color ("fancy"), and distribution ("even"), along with other essential information describing the overall quality. Note the information under "Comments." GIA will also issue reports pertaining to color only.

SOURCE: GIA GEM TRADE LABORATORY, © GEMOLOGICAL INSTITUTE OF AMERICA

Gemstone Report
Expertise de pierre précieuse   No. 35888
Edelstein-Expertise

Weight / Poids / Gewicht	2.046 ct
Cut / Taille / Schliff	octagonal, step cut
Measurements / Dimensions / Masse	7.71 x 7.54 x 4.91 mm
Colour / Couleur / Farbe	purplish red (fancy intense colour)

IDENTIFICATION / IDENTIFIKATION   D I A M O N D
of natural coloration

Comments / Commentaires /   The analysed properties confirm
Bemerkungen   the authenticity of its coloration.

Basel, 17 July 2000 ss

magnification 2.0x   Dr. L. Kiefert, FGA   Prof. Dr. H.A. Hänni, FGA

This report provides essential information related to the color—depth ("Fancy Intense") and origin ("natural")—but there is no information about clarity or cutting. The lab provides more detailed reports, but the owner of this stone requested information pertaining to its color only.

SOURCE: SCHWEIZERISCHES GEMMOLOGISCHES INSTITUT (SWISS GEMMOLOGICAL INSTITUTE)

Here you will find information pertaining to the color, along with overall quality grading. Gübelin will also issue reports on color only.

SOURCE: GÜBELIN GEM LAB (SWISS)

EN 45001
ISO/IEC GUIDE 25
ISO 9002

The HRD Certificates Department is BELTEST accredited for the quality examination of polished diamonds under ref. N° 047.

This certificate may not be reproduced by any means whatsoever unless complete.

colour certificate no.   000000000

The stone in accordance with the above mentioned number has been identified as a natural gem diamond and has the following description:

shape	marquise
weight	0.52 ct
measurements	7.94 x 4.30 x 2.47 mm
luminescence	
lw 366 nm	slight blue
sw 254 nm	nil
colour description	FANCY INTENSE PURPLISH PINK, NATURAL COLOUR
comments	

antwerpen, 11/03/1995

gemmologists

performed examinations

UV luminescence	X
colour charts	X
absorption spectrum	X
luminescence spectrum	
microscopic examination	X
semi-conduction	

colour grade

faint	
light	
intense	X
dark	

colour origin

natural	X
treated	

The here mentioned findings result from scientific measurements and observations carried out in the laboratory of the Diamond High Council and, when necessary, in the "Solid State Physics" laboratory of the University of Antwerp (RUCA).
The decisions are taken according to the knowledge and literature about colour and colour treatment of diamonds known at the time of the examination.

This report was issued to confirm color only—purity, depth, and origin—without information on clarity or cutting. Overall quality reports are also available.

SOURCE: HOGE RAAD VOOR DIAMANT (THE DIAMOND HIGH COUNCIL OF BELGUIM)

This report provides information about color only, but reports including
clarity and cutting are also available upon request.

SOURCE: THE GEM TESTING LABORATORY OF GREAT BRITAIN

Retail Price Guide for Fancy-Color Diamonds*

Prices are per carat in U.S. dollars

C1–C4 TOP LIGHT BROWN

Wt.	FL–VVS	VS	SI	I$_2$
Melee	NA	750–1,200	600–1,200	450–600
¼ ct	NA	750–1,500	675–1,350	600–900
½ ct	NA	825–2,500	750–2,250	600–1,500
¾ ct	NA	900–3,000	900–2,750	675–1,750
1 ct	NA	1,375–4,500	1,500–4,250	900–2,500
2 ct	NA	1,875–5,000	1,750–4,750	1,350–2,750
3 ct	NA	2,625–5,750	2,500–5,500	1,500–3,750
4 ct	NA	3,500–6,250	3,250–6,000	2,500–4,500
5 ct	NA	5,000 7,500	4,750 7,000	3,000 5,000

C5–C7 FANCY LIGHT BROWN TO FANCY BROWN

Wt.	FL–VVS	VS	SI	I$_2$
Melee	NA	600–1,200	525–900	450–750
¼ ct	NA	750–1,650	675–1,500	600–975
½ ct	NA	900–3,000	750–2,500	600–1,750
¾ ct	NA	1,250–3,750	900–3,000	750–2,000
1 ct	NA	1,500–4,500	1,250–4,250	900–2,500
2 ct	NA	2,000–6,250	1,750–5,000	1,250–3,000
3 ct	NA	3,000 7,000	2,500 6,250	1,750–4,750
4 ct	NA	3,750–7,500	3,250–7,000	3,000–5,500
5 ct	NA	7,500–9,000	6,250–8,000	3,750–7,500

FANCY LIGHT YELLOW

Wt.	FL–VVS	VS	SI	I$_2$
Melee	900–1,375	750–1,315	675–1,250	450–1,200
¼ ct	1,625–3,500	1,250–3,000	1,350–2,500	1,200–1,625
½ ct	5,000–6,000	3,750–5,000	3,250–4,500	2,000–2,250
¾ ct	5,750–6,250	5,000–5,750	4,000–4,750	3,000–3,750
1 ct	8,000–9,000	6,250–7,000	5,000–6,250	3,750–5,000
2 ct	9,000–11,000	7,000–8,000	6,600–7,600	6,000–6,600
3 ct	10,000–11,000	8,000–10,000	7,200–8,000	6,400–7,000
4 ct	10,000–11,600	9,000–11,000	8,400–9,400	7,600–8,000
5 ct	13,000–15,000	12,000–14,000	11,000–13,000	9,000–10,000

* Retail prices are based on *The Guide*, Gemworld International, Inc.

FANCY YELLOW

Wt.	FL–VVS	VS	SI	I₂
Melee	1,050–2,250	900–2,000	750–1,875	600–1,625
¼ ct	2,000–4,500	1,750–4,000	1,500–3,750	1,350–3,000
½ ct	5,250–6,500	5,000–6,000	4,250–5,000	3,750–4,250
¾ ct	6,000–7,000	5,750–6,500	5,000–6,250	4,250–5,000
1 ct	7,200–7,600	6,800–7,200	6,400–7,000	5,600–6,000
2 ct	12,000–12,600	10,400–12,000	10,000–11,600	8,000–9,000
3 ct	13,000–14,000	12,000–13,000	10,000–12,000	9,200–9,800
4 ct	14,000–16,000	13,000–15,000	12,000–13,000	10,000–11,000
5 ct	16,000–18,000	15,000–17,000	13,000–15,000	11,000–13,000

FANCY INTENSE YELLOW

Wt.	FL–VVS	VS	SI	I₂
Melee	NA	NA	NA	NA
¼ ct	NA	NA	NA	NA
½ ct	6,800–7,400	6,400–7,000	6,000–6,800	3,500–5,500
¾ ct	9,000–11,000	8,000–10,000	6,600–8,000	6,000–7,000
1 ct	11,400–15,400	11,000–15,000	10,000–13,600	8,000–10,000
2 ct	16,000–17,800	15,600–17,600	13,600–15,200	10,000–12,400
3 ct	18,000–19,000	17,000–18,000	16,000–17,000	11,000–13,000
4 ct	19,000–23,000	18,000–22,000	17,000–20,000	12,000–14,000
5 ct	23,000–26,000	22,000–26,000	20,000–24,000	13,000–15,000

FANCY LIGHT PINK

Wt.	FL–VVS	VS	SI	I₂
Melee	2,250–3,250	2,000–3,000	1,750–2,500	1,625–2,375
¼ ct	7,500–8,000	7,000–7,200	6,250–6,600	5,500–6,000
½ ct	13,000–17,000	11,000–16,000	10,000–12,000	5,000–8,000
¾ ct	30,000–34,000	24,000–30,000	18,000–24,000	12,000–16,000
1 ct	36,000–42,000	32,000–40,000	30,000–36,000	22,000–26,000
2 ct	72,000–90,000	70,000–86,000	60,000–80,000	40,000–50,000
3 ct	110,000–150,000	100,000–140,000	90,000–130,000	60,000–70,000
4 ct	160,000–220,000	150,000–200,000	120,000–140,000	100,000–110,000
5 ct	240,000–260,000	200,000–220,000	160,000–200,000	120,000–160,000

* Retail prices are based on *The Guide*, Gemworld International, Inc.

FANCY PINK

Wt.	FL–VVS	VS	SI	I$_2$
Melee	NA	NA	NA	NA
¼ ct	30,000–60,000	24,000–50,000	22,000–44,000	10,000–20,000
½ ct	70,000–100,000	60,000–90,000	40,000–90,000	20,000–30,000
¾ ct	80,000–110,000	70,000–120,000	50,000–80,000	30,000–40,000
1 ct	120,000–160,000	100,000–140,000	80,000–140,000	50,000–70,000
2 ct	200,000–270,000	150,000–200,000	120,000–180,000	60,000–80,000
3 ct	300,000–500,000	250,000–400,000	180,000–260,000	150,000–200,000
4 ct	350,000–500,000	350,000–450,000	250,000–300,000	170,000–220,000
5 ct	500,000–700,000	400,000–600,000	300,000–600,000	300,000–450,000

FANCY BLUE

Wt.	FL–VVS	VS	SI	I$_2$
Melee	NA	NA	NA	NA
¼ ct	NA	NA	NA	NA
½ ct	120,000–130,000	80,000–120,000	60,000–80,000	40,000–50,000
¾ ct	140,000–160,000	100,000–150,000	80,000–100,000	60,000–70,000
1 ct	240,000–280,000	200,000–240,000	170,000–200,000	140,000–180,000
2 ct	350,000–450,000	300,000–400,000	250,000–350,000	100,000–150,000
3 ct	500,000–750,000	450,000–700,000	400,000–550,000	250,000–350,000
4 ct	600,000–800,000	550,000–750,000	450,000–600,000	300,000–400,000
5 ct	800,000–1,100,000	750,000–1,050,000	600,000–800,000	400,000–500,000

*Retail prices are based on *The Guide*, Gemworld International, Inc.

Prices of Rare Fancy-Color Diamonds Sold at Auction*

Prices are per carat in U.S. dollars

Color	Shape	Size	Color Clarity	Price per Carat
Vivid Blue	oval	5.29	SI$_2$	221,919
Intense Blue	cushion	3.08	VVS$_2$	119,724
Deep Blue	round	1.08	SI$_1$	102,315
Light Blue	heart	5.70	VS$_1$	37,341
Light Gray Blue	marquise	1.08	not graded	17,973
Intense Pink	oval	7.34	VS$_2$	204,149
Intense Orangy Pink	step-cut	13.32	IF	127,069
Orangy Pink	round	4.07	VS$_2$	33,845
Faint Pink	round	1.64	not graded	10,793
Very Light Purple	marquise	4.01	not graded	9,490
Vivid Yellow	oval	1.17	not graded	19,768
Deep Brown Orange	round	3.28	not graded	6,341
Black	marquise	11.48	not graded	2,114
Red	round	.95	I$_2$	1,000,000
Deep Green	cushion	1.65	VS$_2$	386,189

*Prices are compiled from several issues of the *Rapaport Diamond Report*.

Retail Price Guide for Fancy-Color Synthetic Diamonds*

Prices are per carat in U.S. dollars

VIVID INTENSE YELLOW AND YELLOWISH ORANGE

Weight	VVS Range	VS Range	SI Range
0.05–0.14 ct	1,200–2,000	1,000–1,700	900–1,400
0.15–0.24 ct	1,800–2,400	1,500–2,000	1,300–1,700
0.25–0.49 ct	2,600–4,300	2,200–3,600	1,900–3,100
0.50–0.69 ct	3,900–5,800	3,400–4,800	2,900–4,100
0.70–0.89 ct	5,200–7,200	4,500–6,000	3,900–5,100
0.90–0.99 ct	6,500–8,400	5,600–7,000	4,800–6,000
1.00–1.24 ct	7,600–10,100	6,500–8,400	5,700–7,200
1.25–1.49 ct	9,100–12,400	7,800–10,300	6,800–8,900

FANCY LIGHT, MEDIUM, AND INTENSE BLUE

Weight	VVS Range	VS Range	SI Range	I Range
0.05–0.14 ct	4,000–4,800	3,400–4,000	3,000–3,500	2,700–3,100
0.15–0.24 ct	4,400–5,100	3,700–4,200	3,300–3,600	3,000–3,300
0.25–0.49 ct	4,800–6,700	4,100–5,600	3,600–4,800	3,300–4,400
0.50–0.69 ct	6,100–7,800	5,200–6,500	4,500–5,600	4,200–5,000
0.70–0.89 ct	7,000–9,100	6,000–7,500	5,300–6,500	4,800–5,900
0.90–0.99 ct	8,200–10,600	7,000–8,800	6,100–7,600	5,600–6,800
1.00–1.24 ct	9,600–13,200	8,200–1,100	7,100–9,400	6,500–8,500
1.25–1.49 ct	11,900–16,500	10,200–13,700	8,900–11,800	8,100–19,600

FANCY RED, FANCY ORANGY RED, FANCY PURPLISH PINK

Weight	VVS Range	VS Range	SI Range	I Range
0.05–0.14 ct	5,100–6,100	4,400–5,100	3,800–4,400	3,500–3,900
0.15–0.24 ct	5,500–6,400	4,700–5,300	4,100–4,600	3,800–4,100
0.25–0.49 ct	6,000–8,200	5,100–6,800	4,500–5,800	4,100–5,300
0.50–0.69 ct	7,400–9,100	6,300–7,600	5,500–6,500	5,000–5,900
0.70–0.89 ct	8,200–10,700	7,000–8,900	6,100–7,700	5,600–6,900
0.90–0.99 ct	9,600–11,700	8,300–9,700	7,200–8,300	6,600–7,500
1.00–1.24 ct	10,500–13,800	9,000–11,500	7,900–9,900	7,200–8,900
1.25–1.49 ct	12,500–16,700	10,700–13,900	9,300–11,900	8,500–10,800

* Retail prices are based on information provided for Lucent Diamonds' Ultimate Created Diamonds™.

Retail Price Guide for HPHT-Treated Fancy-Color Diamonds*

Prices are per carat in U.S. dollars

FANCY YELLOW

Weight	VVS Range	VS Range
¾ carat	2,300–3,250	2,150–3,000
1 carat	3,600–4,900	3,300–4,400
2 carat	6,500–7,800	6,000–7,200
3 carat	7,500–9,100	6,900–8,400
4 carat	8,800–10,700	8,100–9,800

INTENSE YELLOW

Weight	VVS Range	VS Range
¾ carat	5,000–6,900	4,300–5,700
1 carat	7,300–9,800	6,300–8,200
2 carat	12,800–16,300	10,900–13,500
3 carat	14,700–18,500	12,600–15,400
4 carat	16,700–21,200	14,300–17,600

FANCY YELLOWISH GREEN

Weight	VVS Range	VS Range
¾ carat	2,400–3,350	2,250–3,050
1 carat	3,700–4,300	3,400–4,000
2 carat	6,200–8,000	5,700–7,300
3 carat	7,700–9,800	8,600–8,900
4 carat	9,300–11,800	8,600–10,800

INTENSE YELLOWISH GREEN

Weight	VVS Range	VS Range
¾ carat	4,950–6,850	4,250–5,700
1 carat	7,300–9,800	6,300–8,200
2 carat	12,800–16,400	10,900–13,600
3 carat	14,800–18,900	12,700–15,700
4 carat	17,000–21,900	14,600–18,100

*Retail prices are based on information provided for Lucent Diamonds' Luminari™ diamonds.

PART ◆ THREE

Design & Style:
Getting the Look You Want

CHAPTER THIRTEEN

Choosing the Setting

The setting you choose will be determined primarily by your personal taste. Nevertheless, it is a good idea to be familiar with a few of the most common settings so that you have a working vocabulary and some idea of what is available.

Bezel setting. With a bezel setting, a rim holds the stone and completely surrounds the gem. Bezels can have straight edges, scalloped edges, or any molded shape that accommodates the stone. The backs can be open or closed. One advantage of the bezel setting is that it can make a stone look larger. The bezel setting can also conceal nicks or chips on the girdle and protect the girdle of the stone from chips and nicks.

Bezel-set center stones with "grosgrain textured" platinum and 18K gold

Keep in mind that if you use yellow gold in a bezel setting, the yellow of the bezel surrounding the stone will be reflected into the stone, causing a white stone to appear less white. On the other hand, a yellow gold bezel can make a red stone such as ruby look even redder or an emerald look greener.

A variation on the bezel setting is the collet setting, which has a similar appearance to the bezel setting but involves the use of gold tubing.

Partial bezel-set solitaire

Prong setting. Prong settings are perhaps the most common type of setting. They come in an almost infinite variety. There are four-prong, six-prong, and special styles such as Belcher, Fishtail, and six-prong Tiffany. In addition, prongs can be pointed, rounded, flat, or V-shaped. Extra prongs provide added security for the stone and can

Graceful intertwined prongs
hold these diamonds
in five-stone bands.

V-shaped prongs
protect point of heart.

In this grouping, lower ring
shows gypsy setting; upper
ring shows collet setting.

Channel-set baguettes
in a wedding band

make a stone look slightly larger. However, too many prongs holding too small a stone can overpower the stone, making the stone look smaller and the mounting look heavy. When setting a marquise, heart shape, or pear shape, I recommend that the point or points be held by a V-shaped prong, which will best protect the point(s). For emerald-cut stones that have "canted" corners (a corner with a small diagonal edge rather than forming a 90° angle), flat prongs are the preferred choice.

Gypsy setting. In this type of setting, the metal at the top of the ring (around the stone) is much heavier than the shank. The stone is set flush into a hole at the top.

Illusion setting. The illusion setting is used to make the mounted stone appear larger. There are numerous styles from which to choose.

Flat-top and bead settings. In a flat-top setting, a faceted stone is placed into a hole in the flat top of the metal and then held in place by small chips of metal attached by solder at the stone's girdle. Sometimes these metal chips are worked into small beads, so this setting is sometimes called a bead setting.

Channel setting. This setting is used extensively today, especially for wedding bands. The stones are set into a channel with no metal separating them. In some cases, the channel can continue completely around the ring, so that the piece has a continuous row of stones.

Bar setting. This setting, which resembles a channel setting, combines the contemporary and classic looks. It is used in a circular band, and instead of prongs, each stone is held in the ring by a long thin bar, shared between two stones.

Pavé setting. This setting is used for numerous small stones set together in a cluster with no metal showing through. The impression is that the piece is entirely paved with stones. The setting can be flat or dome-shaped, and can be worked so that the piece almost appears to be one large single stone. Fine pavé work can be very expensive.

Bar-set bands

Cluster setting. A cluster setting usually consists of one large stone and several smaller stones as accents. A cluster setting is designed to create a lovely larger piece from several small stones.

Fine pavé work in diamond and pearl rings and in a band

Distinctive Contemporary Settings

Today there are many interesting and distinctive designs offering something for everyone. Fine casting houses produce top-quality settings that simply await the stones to finish them off. Some firms produce semi-mounts: settings complete with side stones, awaiting only your center stone. These can provide affordable and easy solutions to creating a new ring, or remounting stones from another piece.

An increasing number of custom jewelry designers also cater to today's market (see color section). International jewelry design competitions such as the Spectrum Awards designer competition sponsored by the American Gem Trade Association (AGTA), or the Diamonds-International Awards sponsored by the Diamond Information Center, provide a showcase for their work. The result is an almost limitless choice, ranging from bold sculpted gold and platinum combinations to intricate antique reproductions.

Settings to Suit Your Lifestyle

It is important to consider your lifestyle when selecting any piece of jewelry. Be realistic about the wear and tear a ring or bracelet might take, and remember that no piece of jewelry is indestructible. Remember that even diamond, the hardest natural substance known, can chip or break if exposed to a sharp accidental blow.

Active outdoor types, for example, might be better off avoiding jewelry like a ring containing a marquise or pear-shaped stone, since both these shapes have points. Points are more vulnerable to chipping or breaking, which could result from the kind of sudden or sharp blow an active person might subject a stone to.

In addition, the shank as well as the prongs of a ring will show the effects of wear; any detailing on a ring will blur over time, as the result of gardening, playing on the beach, mountain climbing, handling ski equipment or bicycles, or any other kind of repeated contact or use.

Classic four- or six-prong settings served a less active generation well but may not be as suitable for today's woman. If your daily schedule features a great deal of activity, you would be wise to consider a sturdier jewelry style, keeping in mind that *sturdy* and *graceful* are not mutually exclusive. For example, a bezel setting might be better suited to your activity level. This choice won't detract from a gemstone's brilliance, yet it will afford you and your fine gems greater security.

Since everyday activities can loosen a setting as easily as more strenuous ones can, it is important to have a reputable jeweler check mountings and settings once every six months. Chlorine attacks 14K gold (and lower), soldering links and stress points, so if you swim regularly in a chlorinated pool, take your jewelry off first.

In terms of ring design, while rings are usually round, fingers aren't. Top-heavy rings will turn on the finger unless the diameter, or outline, is square or stirrup-shaped to conform to the shape of the finger. Also, remember that rings worn together side by side quickly begin to wear on each other.

Tips for Selecting the Right Style

1. Set a realistic budget range to eliminate confusion and temptation that can result in disappointment.
2. Shop around and familiarize yourself with current styles to educate your eye and learn what really appeals to you.
3. Try on different styles. Jewelry looks different when you see it *on*.

This holds true of rings especially. I've seen many men and women insist they don't like a particular ring in a showcase, and then love it when they try it on.

4. If you're trying to achieve an impressive look with smaller stones, consider interesting jackets for earrings, or inserts or wraps for rings. These enable you to slip your ring or studs into another piece (usually gold, platinum, or silver, sometimes with stones) and instantly create a larger look.

5. If selecting an engagement ring, remember that you will also be wearing a wedding band. Be sure to select a style that will complement the type of wedding band you are considering.

International Ring Size Equivalents

American	English	French/Japanese	Metric
½	A	–	37.8252
¾	A½	–	38.4237
1	B	–	39.0222
1¼	B½	–	39.6207
1½	C	–	40.2192
1¾	C½	–	40.8177
2	D	1	41.4162
2¼	D½	2	42.0147
2½	E	–	42.6132
2¾	E½	3	43.2117
3	F	4	43.8102
3¼	F½	–	44.4087
3¼	G	5	45.0072
3½	G½	–	45.6057
3¾	H	6	46.2042
4	H½	–	46.8027
4¼	I	7	47.4012
4½	I½	8	47.9997
4¾	J	–	48.5982
5	J½	9	49.1967
5¼	K	10	49.7952
5½	K½	–	50.3937
5¾	L	11	50.9922
6	L½	–	51.5907
6¼	M	12	52.1892
6½	M½	13	52.7877
6¾	N	–	53.4660
7	N½	14	54.1044
7	O	15	54.7428
7¼	O½	–	55.3812
7½	P	16	56.0196
7¾	P½	–	56.6580
8	Q	17	57.2964
8¼	Q½	18	57.9348
8½	R	–	58.5732
8¾	R½	19	59.2116
9	S	20	59.8500
9¼	S½	–	60.4884
9½	T	21	61.1268
9¾	T½	22	61.7652
10	U	–	62.4026
10¼	U½	23	63.0420
10½	V	24	63.6804
10¾	V½	–	64.3188
11	W	25	64.8774
11¼	W½	–	65.4759
11½	X	26	66.0744
11¾	X½	–	66.6729
12	Y	–	67.2714
12¼	Y½	–	67.8699
12½	Z	–	68.4684

PART  FOUR

Important Advice
Before & After You Buy

CHAPTER FOURTEEN

What to Ask
When Buying the Stone

Asking the right questions is the key to knowing what you're getting when it comes to buying diamonds. It is also the only way you can be sure what you are comparing when considering diamonds from different jewelers. Be sure the jeweler can answer your questions or can get the answers for you. Then, be sure the jeweler is willing to put the answers *in writing* on your bill of sale. Finally, verify the facts—double-check that the stone is as represented—by having it examined by a qualified gemologist-appraiser. In this way you'll be able to make an informed choice about quality and value, you'll have no doubt about what you are getting, and you'll begin to develop a solid relationship with the jeweler from whom you make the purchase, based on confidence and trust. And, in the event the stone is not as represented, you'll know in time—and have the information you need—to get your money back.

Questions to Ask When Buying a Diamond

You should always have very specific information before purchasing a fine diamond weighing one carat or more. For smaller stones, the information may not be so readily available, since most jewelers don't take the time to grade them precisely. An experienced jeweler, however, should be able to provide information regarding quality for stones from a half carat and up, or offer to find it for you. Indeed, some laboratories are now providing grading reports for diamonds as small as half a carat or smaller.

Also keep in mind that since it is not possible to grade mounted diamonds accurately, I recommend that fine diamonds weighing one carat or more be purchased unmounted, or removed from the setting and then remounted. In jewelry containing numerous small diamonds, the stones are graded before they are set, and the information may be on the sales tag. If not, it is extremely difficult to know for sure what the true quality is, and much can be concealed by a setting. I recommend buying such pieces only from a knowledgeable jeweler with a good reputation.

Here are the basic questions to ask and the information that needs to be included on the bill of sale of your diamond:

1. *What is the exact carat weight?* Be sure the stone's *weight* is given, not its *spread* (see chapter 8).
2. *What is its color grade?* And what grading system was used? (See chapter 6.) Is the color natural?
3. *What is its clarity (flaw) grade?* Again, ask what system was used (see chapter 7).
4. *What shape is it?* Round, pear, marquise? (See chapter 5.)
5. *Is it well cut for its shape?* How would the make be graded: ideal, excellent, good? (See chapter 5.)
6. *What are the exact millimeter dimensions of the stone?*
7. *Is this stone accompanied by a diamond grading report or certificate?* Ask for the full report (see chapter 9).

Be sure to find out what system was used to grade the stone. If Gemological Institute of America (GIA) terms are used, ask if GIA standards and methods have been applied to grading the stone.

Be sure to get the *exact* millimeter dimensions of the stone; the dimensions can be approximated if the stone is mounted. For a round stone, be sure you are given *two* dimensions for the stone's diameter; since most are not round, you need the highest and lowest dimensions. For fancy shapes, get the dimensions of the length and width. Always get the dimension from the table to the culet as well, that is, the depth of the stone.

Be especially careful if the diamond is being taken out on consignment, on a jeweler's memorandum or sales slip, or on a contingency sale. Having the measurements in writing helps protect you from being accused of switching, should you have to return the stone for any reason.

Always ask if the stone has a certificate or diamond grading report. If so, make sure it accompanies the stone; if you are taking the stone on approval, ask for a copy of the report. If there is no report or certificate, find out who determined the color and flaw grades, make sure the seller puts that information on the bill of sale, and insist that the sale be contingent on the stone's actually having the grades represented.

Additional Questions to Help You Make Your Selection

Is it large enough? This is a valid question and one you should be honest with yourself about. If you think the diamond is too small, you won't feel good about wearing it. Remember that such other factors as clarity and color can be juggled several grades with little visible difference, and this might enable you to get a larger diamond. And remember that the color and type of setting can also help you achieve a larger look.

Does this stone have a good make? Does this stone have good proportions? How do its proportions compare to the "ideal?" Remember, much variance can exist and a stone can still be a beautiful, desirable gem even if it does not conform to the ideal. Nonetheless, you won't want a stone with poor proportions, so if you have any question about the stone's brilliance and liveliness—if it looks lifeless or dull in spots—you should ask specifically about the proportioning of the cut. In addition, you should ask if there are any cutting faults that might make the stone more vulnerable to chipping or breaking, as, for example, an extremely thin girdle would.

Has this stone been clarity enhanced? Be sure to ask whether or not the diamond has been laser treated or fracture-filled (see chapter 7). If it is accompanied by a GIA report, the report will indicate lasering, if present. However, the GIA won't issue a report on a fracture-filled stone, and some jewelers don't know how to detect them. If there is no GIA report, be sure to ask explicitly, and get a statement in writing that the diamond is or is not clarity enhanced, whichever the case may be. Getting this fact in writing may save you a big headache should you learn later that the stone is enhanced.

Does this stone show any fluorescence? If a diamond fluoresces blue when viewed in daylight or under daylight-type fluorescent light, it will appear whiter than it really is. This can be a desirable quality so long as the stone has not been graded or classified incorrectly. A diamond may also fluoresce yellow, which means that in certain lights its color could appear worse than it actually is. If the stone has a diamond grading report, any fluorescence will be indicated there. If there is no report, and if the jeweler can't tell you whether or not the stone exhibits any fluorescence, the stone's color grade may be incorrect.

Special Tips When Buying a Diamond

Ask the Jeweler to Clean the Stone

Don't hesitate to ask to have the stone cleaned before you examine it. Cleaning will remove dirt, grease, or indelible purple ink. Cleaning is best done by steaming or in an ultrasonic cleaner. Cleaning also helps to ensure that you'll see the full beauty of the stone; diamonds can become very dirty just from customers handling them and, as a result, look less brilliant and sparkling than they really are.

View the Stone Against a Dead-White Background

When looking at unmounted stones, look at them only against a *dead white background* such as white blotter paper or a white business card, or on a grading trough. Examine the stone against the white background so that you are looking at it through the side, not down through the table (see chapter 6). Tilt the stone toward a good light source; a daylight fluorescent lamp is best. If the stone shows any yellow body tint when viewed through the girdle, if it is not as colorless as an ice cube, then the diamond is not white or colorless.

Get the Facts on a Bill of Sale

Ask that all the facts concerning the stone be put on the bill of sale. These include the carat weight, the color and flaw grades, the cut, and the dimensions. Also, be sure you obtain the report on any certificated stone, as diamonds accompanied by laboratory reports are sometimes called.

Other information that should be included for jewelry. If the piece is being represented as being made by a famous designer or house (Van Cleef and Arpels, Tiffany, Caldwell, Cartier, etc.) and the price reflects this, the name of the designer or jewelry firm should be stated on the bill of sale. If the piece is represented as antique (technically, an antique must be at least a hundred years old) or as a period piece from a popular, collectible period like Art Deco, Art Nouveau, or Edwardian (especially if made by a premier artisan of the period), this information should be stated on the bill of sale, with the approximate age or date of manufacture and a statement describing the condition. If the piece is made by hand, or custom designed, this should be indicated on the bill of sale. If the piece is to be taken on approval, make sure millimeter dimensions—top to bottom, as well as length, width, or diameter—are provided, as well as a full description of the piece. Also, check that a time period is indicated, such as "two days." Before you sign anything, be sure that you are signing an approval form and not a binding contract for purchase.

Verify Facts with a Gemologist

If a stone is one carat or larger and is not accompanied by a respected laboratory report, make the sale contingent on verification of the facts by a qualified gemologist, gem-testing lab, or the GIA. While the GIA will not estimate dollar value, it will verify color, flaw grade, make, fluorescence, weight, and other physical characteristics.

Weigh the Facts

Decide what is important to you, and then weigh the facts. Most people think color and make are the most important considerations when buying a diamond, but if you want a larger stone, you may have to come down several grades in color, or choose a slightly spread stone, or select one of the new shapes that look much larger than traditional cuts. The most important thing is to know what you're getting, and get what you pay for.

CHAPTER FIFTEEN

How to Select a Reputable Jeweler & Gemologist Consultant

It's very difficult to give advice on this matter, since there are so many exceptions to any rules I can suggest. Size and years in business are not always absolute indicators of the reliability of a firm. Some one-person jewelry firms are highly respected; others are not. Some well-established firms that have been in business for many years have built their trade on the highest standards of integrity and knowledge; others should have been put out of business years ago.

One point worth stressing is that for the average consumer, price alone is not a reliable indicator of the integrity or knowledge of the seller. Aside from variations in quality, which often are not readily discernible by the consumer, significant price differences can also result from differences in jewelry manufacturing processes. Many jewelry manufacturers sell mass-produced lines of good-quality jewelry to jewelers all across the country. Mass-produced items, many of which are beautiful, classic designs, are usually much less expensive than handmade, one-of-a-kind pieces, or those on which there is a limited production. The work of some designers may be available in only a few select establishments and may carry a premium because of skill, labor, reputation, and limited distribution. Handmade or one-of-a-kind pieces are always more expensive, since the initial cost of production is paid by one individual rather than shared by many, as in mass-produced pieces.

Furthermore, depending on the store, retail markups also vary based on numerous factors unique to each retailer, including differences in insurance coverage, security costs, credit risks, education and training costs, special services such as in-house design and custom jewelry production and repair, customer service policies, and more.

The best way to select wisely is by shopping around. Go to several fine jewelry firms in your area and compare the services they offer, how knowledgeable the salespeople seem, the quality of their products, and pricing for specific items. This will give you a sense of what is fair in your market area. As you do so, however, remember to ask the right questions to be sure the items are truly comparable, and pay attention to design and manufacturing differences as well. As part of this process, it may be helpful to consider these questions:

- *How long has the firm been in business?* A quick check with the Better Business Bureau may reveal whether or not there are significant consumer complaints.
- *What are the gemological credentials of the jeweler, manager, or owner?* Is there a gemologist on staff? Does the store have its own laboratory?
- *What special services are provided?* Are custom design services, rare or unusual gemstones, educational programs, Gemprint, or photographic services for your jewelry available?
- *How would you describe the store window?* Is the jewelry nicely displayed? Or is the window a mélange of incredible bargains and come-on advertising to lure you in?
- *How would you describe the overall atmosphere?* Is the sales staff's manner professional, helpful, tasteful? Or hustling, pushy, intimidating?
- *What is the store's policy regarding returns?* Full refund or only store credit? How many days? What basis for return?
- *What is the repair or replacement policy?*
- *Will the firm allow a piece to be taken "on approval"?* It won't hurt to ask. Some jewelers will. However, unless you know the jeweler personally this is not often permitted today, since too many jewelers have suffered from stolen, damaged, or switched merchandise.
- *To what extent will the firm guarantee its merchandise to be as represented?* Be careful here. Make sure you've asked the right questions, and get complete and accurate information on the bill of sale, or you may find yourself stuck because of a technicality.

If the jeweler can't or won't provide the necessary information, I recommend that you go to another store, no matter how much you've fallen in love with the piece. If you're making the purchase on a contingency basis, put the terms of the contingency on the bill of sale.

Never allow yourself to be intimidated into accepting anyone's claims. Beware of the person who says "Just trust me" or who tries to intimidate you with statements such as "Don't you trust me?" A trustworthy jeweler will not have to ask for your trust; he or she will earn it through knowledge, reliability, and a willingness to give you any information you request—in writing.

Again, in general, you will be in a stronger position to differentiate between a knowledgeable, reputable jeweler and one who isn't if you've shopped around first. Unless you are an expert, visit several firms, ask questions, examine merchandise carefully, and then you be the judge.

Using a Gemologist Consultant

Somewhat new to the gem and jewelry field is the arrival of the gemologist consultant. People interested in acquiring a very fine diamond, a fancy-color diamond, or fine piece of period or antique jewelry that may be difficult to find in traditional jewelry stores are now seeking the professional services of experienced gemologist consultants. A gemologist consultant can provide a variety of services, including general consulting to help you determine what you really want, what it will cost, and how to best acquire it; how to dispose of jewelry you already own, or from an estate; how to design or redesign a piece of jewelry and have it made. A gemologist consultant can also provide the expertise needed to help you safely purchase diamonds or jewelry at auction, or from private estate sales. An experienced gemologist consultant can expand your view of the possibilities in terms of diamonds and also suggest ways to make jewelry more personal and distinctive.

As with all else in the sparkling world of diamonds and jewelry, be sure to check the credentials of anyone offering services as a gemologist consultant. Do they have a gemological diploma? How long have they been working in the field of gems? Do they have a laboratory? Can they provide references within the field? Can they provide client references? If you have jewelry you wish to sell, arrange meetings at a safe place, such as a bank vault.

Fees vary, depending on the gemologist consultant's level of expertise and experience and the nature of the assignment. For example, for general consulting about how to buy or sell diamonds or jewelry, you should expect to pay about $125 to $200 per hour for someone with good credentials.

For assistance in the acquisition or sale of specific gems or pieces of jewelry, some gemologist consultants work on a fixed fee for the project, some on a percentage of the purchase or sale amount, and some at an hourly rate. When I am retained by clients, my work is done on one of the bases noted above, or even a combination of them, depending on the nature of the work to be done and what best meets the client's needs.

If You Want to File a Complaint

If you have a complaint about a firm's practices or policies, please contact the Better Business Bureau in your city. In addition, if any jeweler has misrepresented what was sold to you, please contact the Jeweler's Vigilance Committee (JVC), 25 West 45th Street, Suite 400, New York, NY 10036, (212) 997-2002. This group can provide invaluable assistance to you, investigate your complaint, and take action against firms believed to be guilty of fraudulent activity in the jewelry industry.

CHAPTER SIXTEEN

Buying on the Internet:
E-Commerce & Online Auctions

E-commerce is the current buzzword, and diamond and jewelry websites are springing up almost daily, along with online auction sites. The internet offers an endless array of merchandise from around the world—a virtual international flea market—and opens doors to more choices than ever imagined, at prices often represented to be much lower than what can be found in traditional jewelry stores. Buying on the internet can be fun, and there are some good opportunities for knowledgeable buyers, possibly even a real "treasure" at a bargain price. But e-commerce and online auctions are not for everyone, and the risk of buying something that is not properly represented is very high. Before flying off into cyberspace, take a few moments to consider some of the pros and cons.

For many, the major attraction of shopping on-line is convenience. It is fast and easy, enabling you to make decisions in private, but without the assistance of salespeople. For those who live in remote areas far from fine jewelry stores, it provides an opportunity to see what is available, see what's new and exciting, and keep current about everything from gemstones to the latest award-winning designers. Many online vendors also provide educational sites to help you understand more about what you are buying. And for people who leave important gifts to the last minute, the internet can bring the world of jewelry directly to the screen, in time to be a real lifesaver!

It is easy to see the allure of internet shopping, but in all too many cases it is not all that it appears to be. Where diamonds and jewelry are concerned, the disadvantages may quickly outweigh the advantages, especially on auction sites.

The first disadvantage is the inability to see and compare diamonds and jewelry firsthand. As I hope you've learned from previous chapters, this is a serious shortcoming, since it is impossible to accurately judge beauty and desirability from a static photo. Furthermore, you can't determine how well made a piece of jewelry might be or how it might compare with the alternatives. Be sure to ask about the vendor's return policy, and read the fine print. Find out how quickly merchandise must be returned and whether you will receive a refund. Be leery of vendors who will only give a credit toward future purchases.

Another serious problem is the absence of any screening mechanism to help you determine the reliability of information provided. Sales information pertaining to diamonds or jewelry being sold is often incomplete and inaccurate, and many "educational" sites are also filled with inaccurate, incomplete, or misleading information. It is also difficult to find reliable information about the competence or trustworthiness of many online vendors, and written representations may be meaningless unless you can work out a way to verify the facts before making payment to the vendor.

In general, everything I have warned about in previous chapters applies to purchases from an online vendor or auction. As I have stressed repeatedly, many of the factors affecting quality and value cannot be accurately judged without gemological training, experience, and proper equipment, and many online vendors are so deficient in requisite knowledge and skill that their representations may be unreliable.

I cannot emphasize too strongly the importance of taking every precaution to protect yourself and ensure you are getting what you think you are getting, at an appropriate price. Remember that many internet companies and individual vendors are unknown entities, without reliable track records or well-established reputations. This means that problems might be more difficult or impossible to resolve satisfactorily, regardless of "guarantees" made before purchase. You must also remember that it may be difficult or impossible to find the seller off-line, and you cannot rely on vendor ratings because they can be easily rigged by the unscrupulous.

Appraisals and Laboratory Reports
Provide a False Sense of Security

Appraisals and gem-testing laboratory reports are being used increasingly by online sellers to increase confidence among prospective buyers.

Unfortunately, they are also being used increasingly by the unscrupulous. I am seeing an increase in bogus appraisals and fraudulent lab reports that have duped unsuspecting buyers into purchasing something that has been misrepresented. I have also seen diamonds accompanied by reports from highly respected labs, where the quality of the stone does not match the description on the report. Be sure to get independent verification of any documentation provided by the seller (see chapter 10), before payment if possible.

Remember also that you cannot properly judge a gem on the basis of a lab report or appraisal alone. I've seen many diamonds with "great reports" that were not beautiful (and should sell for less than one might surmise based on the report alone), and others with "questionable" reports that were exceptionally beautiful (and should cost more than the report would indicate). In other words, you really must see the stone along with the report.

Other problems that are surfacing on the web include the following:

- *Failure to comply with Federal Trade Commission (FTC) guidelines.* The FTC has found extensive failure to comply with FTC guidelines. Most notably, descriptions provided by sellers often omit critical information pertaining to quality factors, exact weight, and treatments used on diamonds.
- *Prices are often higher than fair retail.* Don't assume you will pay a lower price, and beware of fictitious "comparative retail" prices that lead you to believe you are getting a bargain. Prices are often no lower than those at a local jewelry store, and many e-retailers sell jewelry at prices significantly higher than what you would pay for comparable quality from knowledgeable, independent jewelers. Before buying on-line, check prices from a variety of sources, including your local jeweler.
- *"Wholesale" claims may be misleading.* "Wholesale" online offerings present even greater risks to consumers than buying in any wholesale jewelry district (see chapter 10), because you do not see the actual diamond or jewelry firsthand and have no guarantee you are buying from a bona fide wholesaler. Many people buying "wholesale" through online sources are not getting the bargains they believe they are getting, and many mistakes would have been avoided had the buyer seen the jewelry first or had an opportunity to compare it with alternatives.

In some cases, arrangements can be made to allow you to view the stone before the vendor receives payment, using a local bank or gemological laboratory, for example, as an intermediary. I recommend this be done wherever possible.

- *Here today, gone tomorrow.* In numerous reported cases, buyers have never received the merchandise for which they paid, or received merchandise that was not as represented. Often there is no recourse because vendors cannot be located once the transaction is complete.

Online Auctions—Rewards and Rip-Offs

Fine auction houses are an important source of exquisite jewelry from bygone eras, often exhibiting elaborate workmanship that cannot be duplicated today. They are also an important source of some of the finest, rarest, and most magnificent natural gemstones—gems that surpass even the best material being mined today—which are no longer available in the jewelry trade. Such gems may fetch handsome prices—possibly even a new record—or some knowledgeable buyer may recognize a treasure that others have missed and pay very little. This, for many, is what makes the auction arena so fascinating.

Items offered at auction may also come to the auction block to settle estates, or as a means to dispose of unclaimed property, and usually must be sold at whatever the highest bid might be, regardless of value. While this is no guarantee that you'll get a bargain, because knowledgeable buyers know the value of pieces on which they are bidding, sometimes these pieces are sold at very low prices because no one obtained proper certification and they get overlooked, even by the pros!

Buying at auction can be a rewarding experience, but keep in mind that even at the best firms there is an element of risk. One must be very knowledgeable, or work with an expert consultant, to recognize opportunities and spot pitfalls. Over the years I've seen many pieces acquired from reputable auction firms that contained synthetic stones, fracture-filled diamonds, and diffusion-treated sapphires.

As I have stressed throughout this book, no one can properly judge any fine gem without seeing it firsthand and examining it with proper gem-testing equipment. Where auctions are concerned, proper examination is even more critical because the auction house has limited liability.

I never bid on any item at auction without having personally viewed the piece and examined it with proper gem-testing equipment. Firms such as Antiquorum, Christie's, and Sotheby's provide opportunities to view the items at exhibitions held at various locations around the country before the auction, and bidding takes place both on-site and on-line, as a convenience to people who cannot be present. However, this is not the case with all online auction sites, and in many cases there is no opportunity to view the item before bidding on it. In such cases, more than anything else, success is dependent upon having incredible luck!

Protection May Be Illusion

Where some auction sites are concerned, you may be under the impression that you are protected against misrepresentation and have recourse should there be a problem, but this may be just an illusion. In reality, you may have no recourse at all. Never forget that in situations where proper examination is not possible, the risk is dramatically increased: you are bidding on a blind item from a blind source. Even among legitimate sources, not seeing the diamond or jewelry before purchase can result in disappointment when you receive your purchase. Be sure to read the "terms and conditions" very carefully, especially the fine print pertaining to "representations, warranties, and limits of liability."

I was recently contacted by a woman regarding a diamond purchased from an individual through an online auction site. She had previously purchased a diamond through an internet auction, and arranged for us to confirm that the diamond was properly represented before she paid for it. She did very well, and obtained a very nice diamond at a price comparable to legitimate wholesale. In the second case, she thought she had arranged a similar transaction. She was very excited about the diamond, which she thought she had purchased at a "bargain" price. She expected to be able to confirm the quality, as she had in the earlier transaction, before paying for it. Here is where the problem began.

The diamond was described as having a certain color, clarity, and weight, but it was not accompanied by any lab report or appraisal. The buyer was aware of this when she bid, but she had been told by the seller that she could have it verified by a third party. She became alarmed and suspicious when the seller would not accept a credit card or agree to an escrow arrangement, especially since she, the buyer, was willing to pay all costs related to the escrow arrangement or credit card fee. The seller had agreed that the buyer could send the stone to a third party for verification, but what was never made clear before the bidding was that the seller would send the stone to a third party only *after* receiving full payment!

I tried to be helpful, but when I spoke with the owner, I also became very suspicious. I asked the owner how she was able to provide such a precise description of the diamond without any appraisal or lab report, and she responded that she knew "by looking." So I asked her if she was a gemologist or in the jewelry trade and I was told no, but that she had looked at "hundreds of diamonds" and "knew what she was looking at." She then told me she was "a lawyer" and began her litany about the buyer having entered into a legally binding contract, and that the buyer knew before bidding that the description was only her "opinion," and so on. I quickly realized that this woman was an experienced "pro" who knew how to legally exploit the auction arena ... and the unsuspecting.

To sum it all up, the seller used the "terms and conditions, warranty and limits of liability" clauses established by the auction site to construct a situation in which she was able to rip off the inexperienced. She knew that representations made in the auction arena without documentation are not guarantees and fall outside the legal constraints placed on other online vendors, and once payment had been received, she had no intention of ever refunding one penny, regardless of what any independent evaluation revealed.

Buying at auction can be an exciting and exhilarating experience with compelling financial incentives, but there are always risks for the unknowledgeable, and buying through online auction sites poses even greater risk. The FTC has warned that internet auction fraud has become a significant problem. According to the FTC, most consumer complaints center on these situations:

- Sellers who don't deliver goods
- Sellers who deliver something far less valuable than they described
- Sellers who don't deliver in a timely way
- Sellers who fail to disclose all the relevant information about the product or terms of sale

Form of Payment May Provide Protection

There are several payment options that might provide some protection. Credit cards offer the most consumer protection, usually including the right to seek a credit through the credit card issuer if the product isn't as delivered. If the seller won't agree, other options include setting up an escrow arrangement (for which there is usually a nominal fee) or using a reliable third party for verification, such as a well-known gem-testing laboratory, before an exchange of products or money.

To sum up, whether you are buying or selling diamonds or jewelry on-line—from e-retailers, auction sites, or individuals—the rewards may be great, but the risks are much higher than buying from traditional sources. For additional information on how to reduce the risk in buying or selling on-line, or to file a complaint, write to the Federal Trade Commission, Consumer Response Center, 600 Pennsylvania Avenue, NW, Washington, DC 20580, or see their website: www.ftc.gov.

Online Sources of Information

There are many sources of online information but no screening mechanism to separate reliable from unreliable information. Consider the source and be wary of information provided by sellers of gems or jewelry. The following sites may provide helpful information:

1. www.ftc.gov (Federal Trade Commission)
2. www.jewelryinfo.org (Jewelry Information Center)
3. www.gia.edu (Gemological Institute of America educational site)
4. www.diamondregistry.com (diamond industry newsletter with consumer information)
5. www.ags.org (American Gem Society)

CHAPTER SEVENTEEN

Choosing the Appraiser & Insurer

Why Is It Important to Get an Appraisal?

If you have bought a diamond or diamond jewelry, getting a professional appraisal and keeping it updated is critical. An appraisal is necessary for four reasons: (1) to verify the facts about the jewelry you have purchased (especially important with the abundance of new synthetic materials and treatments); (2) to obtain adequate insurance to protect against theft, loss, or damage; (3) to establish adequate information to legally claim jewelry recovered by the police; and (4) if items are lost or stolen, to provide sufficient information to make sure they are replaced with jewelry that actually is of comparable quality, if that is what your insurance policy provides.

The need for appraisal services has increased greatly because of the high incidence of theft and sharp increases in the prices of diamonds. It has become necessary to have any fine gem properly appraised, particularly before a purchase decision, given today's costs and the potential for financial loss if the gem is not accurately represented.

It is also important, given recent rising prices, to update value estimations from old appraisals. This will ensure adequate coverage should gems that have been in your possession for several years or more be lost or stolen. In addition, current and accurate appraisals may be needed in connection with inheritance taxes, gifts, or the determination of your net worth.

How to Find a Reliable Appraiser

The appraisal business has been booming over the past few years, and many jewelry firms have begun to provide the service themselves. I must point out, however, that there are essentially no officially established guidelines for going into the gem appraising business. Anyone can represent himself or herself as an appraiser. While many highly qualified professionals are in the business, some others lack the expertise to offer these services. So it is essential to select an appraiser with care and diligence. Further, if the purpose of the appraisal is to verify the identity or genuineness of a gem as well as its value, I recommend that you deal with someone who is in the business of gem identification and appraising and not primarily in the business of selling gems.

To find a reliable gem-testing laboratory, see the appendix for a selected list of laboratories that issue internationally recognized reports. To find a reliable gemologist-appraiser in your community, contact:

The American Society of Appraisers
P.O. Box 17265, Washington, DC 20041
(703) 478-2228 • Ask for a list of *Master Gemologist Appraisers.*

The American Gem Society Laboratory (AGSL)
8881 W. Sahara Ave., Las Vegas, NV 89117
(702) 255-6500 • Ask for a list of *Certified Gemologist Appraisers or Independent Certified Gemologist Appraisers.*

The Accredited Gemologists Association
888 Brannan St., Ste. 1175, San Francisco, CA 94103
(415) 252-9340 • Ask for a list of *Certified Gem Laboratories or Certified Master Gemologists.*

The International Society of Appraisers
16040 Christensen Rd., Ste. 320, Seattle, WA 98188-2929
(206) 241-0359 • Ask for a list of *Certified Appraisers of Personal Property.*

National Association of Jewelry Appraisers
P.O. Box 6558, Annapolis, MD 21401-0558
(410) 897-0889 • Ask for a list of *Certified Master Appraisers or Certified Senior Members.*

In addition, when selecting a gemologist-appraiser, keep the following suggestions in mind:

- *Obtain the names of several appraisers and then compare their credentials.* To be a qualified gemologist-appraiser requires extensive formal training and experience. You can conduct a preliminary check by telephoning the appraisers and inquiring about their gemological credentials.
- *Look for specific credentials.* The Gemological Institute of America (GIA) and the Gemmological Association of Great Britain provide internationally recognized diplomas. GIA's highest award is G.G. (Graduate Gemologist) and the Gemmological Association of Great Britain awards the F.G.A.—Fellow of the Gemmological Association (F.G.A.A. in Australia; F.C.G.A., Canada). Some hold this honor "With Distinction." In Germany, the D.G.G. is awarded; in Asia, the A.G. Make sure the appraiser you select has one of these gemological diplomas. In addition, when seeking an *appraiser,* look for the title C.G.A. (Certified Gemologist Appraiser), which is awarded by the American Gem Society (AGS), or M.G.A. (Master Gemologist Appraiser), which is awarded by the American Society of Appraisers. Some fine gemologists and appraisers lack these titles because they do not belong to the organizations awarding them, but these titles currently represent the highest awards presented in the gemological appraisal field. Anyone holding these titles should have fine gemological credentials and adhere to high standards of professional conduct.
- *Check the appraiser's length of experience.* In addition to formal training, to be reliable a gemologist-appraiser needs extensive experience in the handling of gems, use of the equipment necessary for accurate identification and evaluation, and activity in the marketplace. The appraiser should have at least several years' experience in a well-equipped laboratory.
- *Ask where the appraisal will be conducted.* An appraisal should normally be done in the presence of the customer, if possible. This is important in order to ensure that the same stone is returned to you and to protect the appraiser against charges of "switching." Recently I appraised an old platinum engagement ring that had over twenty years' filth compacted under the high, filigree-type box mounting typical of the early 1920s. After cleaning, which was difficult, the diamond showed a definite brown tint, easily seen by the client, which she had never noticed when the ring was dirty. She had just inherited the ring from her deceased mother-in-law, who had told her it had a blue-white color. If she had

not been present when this ring was being cleaned and appraised, it might have resulted in a lawsuit, for she would certainly have suspected a switch. This particular situation does not present itself often, but appraisers and customers alike need to be diligent and watchful.

If there are several pieces, the process can be very time-consuming. It normally takes about a half hour per item to get all of the specifications, and it can take much longer in some cases. Several appointments may be required for a proper job.

Appraisal Fees

This is a touchy and complex subject. As with any professional service, there should be a suitable charge. Fees should be conspicuously posted or offered readily on request so that the customer knows beforehand what to expect to pay for this service. Fees are essentially based on the expertise of appraisers and the time required of them, as well as the secretarial work required to put the appraisal in written form, since all appraisals should be done in writing. While it used to be standard practice to base appraisal fees on a percentage of the appraised value, this practice is no longer acceptable. Today, all recognized appraisal associations in the United States recommend that fees be based on a flat hourly rate, or on a per-carat charge for diamonds.

There is usually a minimum appraisal fee, regardless of value. The hourly rate charged by a professional, experienced gemologist-appraiser can range from $50 to $150, depending on the complexity of the work to be performed and the degree of expertise required. Find out beforehand what the hourly rate is and what the minimum fee will be.

For certification or special gemological consulting that requires special expertise, rates can easily be $125 to $150 per hour. Extra services such as photography, radiography, Gemprint, or spectroscopic examination of fancy-color diamonds will require additional fees.

Be wary of appraisal services offering appraisals at very low rates and of appraisers who continue to base their fee on a percentage of the "appraised valuation." The Internal Revenue Service, for example, will not accept appraisals performed by appraisers who charge a percentage-based fee.

Some appraisers can photograph jewelry, which I suggest. On the photo, the appraiser should note the approximate magnification and the date, along with your name as the owner. This provides a means of identifying merchandise that may have been stolen or lost and subsequently recovered by police. The photo can also be useful with the U.S. Customs Service should you take your jewelry with you on a trip outside the United States and find yourself having to prove that the jewelry was not purchased abroad.

Choosing an Insurer

Once you have a complete appraisal, the next step is to obtain adequate insurance. Most people do not realize that insurers differ widely in their coverage and reimbursement or replacement procedures. Many companies will not reimburse the "full value" provided in the policy, but instead exercise a "replacement" option by which they offer a *cash sum less than the amount for which the jewelry is insured,* or offer to replace it for you. Therefore, it is important to ask very specific questions to determine the precise coverage offered. I recommend asking at least the following:

- How do you satisfy claims? Do you reimburse the insured amount in cash? If not, how is the amount of the cash settlement determined? Or do you replace the jewelry?
- What involvement do I have in the replacement of an item? What assurance do I have that the replacement will be of comparable quality and value to the original?
- What is your coverage on articles that cannot be replaced?
- Exactly what risks does my policy cover? All risks? Mysterious disappearance? At all times?
- Does the policy have any geographic restrictions?
- Are there any exemptions or exclusions? What if the loss involves negligence?
- What are the deductibles, if any?
- What documentation do you expect me to provide?

To help with insurance claims, keep a photo inventory of your jewelry. Take a photo and store it in a safe place (a bank safe deposit box). In case of theft or fire, a photo will be useful in helping you describe your jewelry, and also in remembering other pieces that are missing, and in identifying them if recovered. A photo is also useful for insurance documentation. In addition, when planning a trip, whatever jewelry you will be taking should be photographed. Just put it on a table and take a snapshot.

CHAPTER EIGHTEEN

Caring for Your Diamond Jewelry

A key to enjoying your jewelry over the years is knowing how to care for it and protect it. I've come to realize, however, that most people don't know what proper care means. So, here are some tips to help you derive even greater pleasure from your diamonds and jewelry—after you buy!

Store Jewelry Carefully

Keep jewelry pieces separated from each other to prevent scratching. Keep fine jewelry in soft pouches or wrapped in soft cloth to help protect it.

Don't overcrowd your jewelry box. This can result in misplacing or losing pieces that might fall unnoticed from the case. Forcing jewelry into the box may cause damage, such as bending a fragile piece.

Handle and Wear Diamond Jewelry with Care

Every twelve to eighteen months have a reliable jeweler check each fine jewelry piece to make sure the setting is secure, especially the prongs. If you ever feel (or hear) the stone moving in the setting, it's a warning that a prong or bezel needs tightening. Failure to fix this may result in loss or damage to the stone.

Get into the habit of removing jewelry before showering or bathing. Soap can deposit a film that can diminish the liveliness and beauty of diamonds, and necessitate more frequent cleaning. Also, remove jewelry before putting on makeup or powder, and wash your hands after applying makeup (to remove dulling residues) before handling your jewelry.

Never wear diamonds mounted in 14K gold (or lower) in chlorinated swimming pools, or soak your diamond and gold jewelry in chlorine bleach. Chlorine attacks the gold and weakens it, possibly resulting in lost stones.

Avoid wearing fine jewelry while doing any type of rough work, especially where abrasives or chemicals are used. Abrasives can scratch your jewelry—both softer stones used to offset a diamond and the metal in settings. Chemicals such as chlorine and ammonia can cause discoloration of metals used in settings and dull the polish on many stones (necessitating having the stone repolished to restore its full beauty). Chlorine can cause some settings to pit and discolor.

Avoid exposing fine jewelry to intense heat (for example, while *cooking).* Exposure to extreme heat—from contact with a hot pot handle or from getting too near a flame or hot steam—can cause damage to many gems. *Note:* enamel may be ruined by contact with heat. I know someone who ruined an antique diamond ring that had lovely enameling on the shank, by picking up a pot with a handle that was too hot—the enamel came into contact with the handle and melted.

Avoid storing diamond jewelry that contains other gemstones in safe deposit boxes for extended periods of time. While diamonds, rubies, and sapphires won't be adversely affected, other gems—such as opal and emerald—may suffer from the extreme dryness. With these gems, if long-term storage in a safe deposit box or bank vault is unavoidable, place a damp cloth in the box with the jewelry (check from time to time to be sure the cloth is still damp).

A Few Special Words about Rings

Try not to touch the stones in your rings when putting them on or taking them off. Instead, take rings on and off by grasping the metal portion that encircles the finger (called the shank). Slipping rings on and off by grasping the metal shank rather than the stones will prevent a greasy buildup on the stone's surface, which greatly reduces the brilliance and sparkle of a stone.

To keep rings sparkling, get into the habit of "huffing" them. This is a little trick we use to remove the dirt and oily film on the stone's surface (which occurs from putting rings on and off incorrectly, or from occasionally fingering them—which most of us do without even realizing). Each time the stones are touched, a layer of oily film is applied to the top, and the stone's beauty is reduced. To restore its sparkle, simply hold the ring close to your mouth and "huff" on it with your breath—you'll see the stone fog up—and wipe it off with a soft, lint-free cloth, such as a handkerchief, scarf, or coat/blouse sleeve. You'll be amazed to see how much better jewelry can look simply by removing even the lightest film of oil from the surface!

Don't take rings off and lay them on the side of the sink unless you are sure the drain is closed. Also, never remove your rings to wash your hands when away from home (all-too-many have been forgotten and lost).

Take Extra Precautions When Traveling

If you take jewelry with you when traveling, don't pack it in luggage that you plan to check or in luggage to be given to the bell captain at a hotel or a ship's porters, etc. Keep it with you.

Never leave jewelry in your hotel room. Wherever possible, obtain a safety deposit box in which to store your jewelry, even for part of a day. Be wary of in-room safes that are operated by programming your own private code; professionals can quickly and easily override your code and remove the contents of the safe.

Purchase a "body pouch" that can be concealed under clothing for when you *must* carry a valuable piece. Never go sightseeing with valuables in a purse or pocket.

For customs purposes, it can be useful to take a photo (a simple Polaroid) of the jewelry pieces you take with you. Have the photo dated and notarized before departure, so you can prove that you did not purchase it abroad. Otherwise you may be asked to pay duty on it.

Keep a Photo Inventory of your jewelry. You don't need professional photos; simply lay your jewelry out on a flat surface and take several snapshots. They will be invaluable should there be a robbery, providing detectives with a visual record that will make it easier to recognize the stolen pieces and claim what is yours should the jewelry ever be recovered. Photos are also important for insurance purposes and can aid in replacement. Where a piece is one-of-a-kind, and you want to have someone make a replica, a photo can provide a custom jeweler with the necessary details in order to duplicate it.

How to Clean Your Jewelry

Keeping your diamond jewelry clean is essential if you want it to sparkle to its fullest. Film from lotions, powders, and your own skin oils will dull stones and reduce their brilliance. You will be amazed at how much a slight film can affect the brilliance of your gems. So, learn how to keep them clean, and clean them on a regular basis.

The simplest and easiest way to clean any kind of jewelry is simply to wash it with warm sudsy water. Prepare a small bowl of warm sudsy water, using any kind of *mild* liquid detergent. Soak the piece a few minutes and then brush gently with an eyebrow brush or soft toothbrush, keeping the piece submerged in the sudsy water. Rinse thoroughly under running water (make sure the drain is closed—some prefer to place jewelry in a wire strainer before placing under the running water) and pat dry with a soft lint-free cloth or paper towel.

Diamond jewelry pieces that do not contain any other gemstones can be immersed in a solution of equal parts of hot water (not boiling— you should be able to put your fingers in it without pain!) and ammonia. This can be especially effective at removing built up dirt and grime. Let the jewelry soak for a few minutes, brush gently, rinse well, and pat dry with a lint-free cloth. Remember, however, that ammonia should *not* be used on most other gems, and washing with warm, sudsy water is usually sufficient for *all* gemstones.

Never boil jewelry to clean it. Many stones will crack or lose their color.

Use Jewelry Cleaners and Ultrasonic Cleaners with Caution

Commercial jewelry cleaners usually are no more effective than the methods suggested above. They seem to be popular because they are convenient. In any case, *never soak diamond jewelry that contains other gemstones in commercial cleaners for more than a few minutes.* Leaving stones such as emerald or amethyst in some commercial cleaners for any length of time can cause etching of the surface, which reduces the stone's luster (shine). *Never use commercial cleaners containing ammonia or harsh chemicals on diamond jewelry that contains pearls.* For difficult pieces, try the new *ionic* cleaners. These are safe for all gems and are fast, convenient, and affordable.

Diamonds can also be cleaned using an ultrasonic cleaner. However, *I do not recommend ultrasonic cleaning for most gems*—the new ionic cleaners are safer and equally effective. Washing in sudsy water or using an ionic cleaner is simple, effective, and safe for all jewelry.

Protecting Your Diamond with Gemprint™

Gemprint is a unique service offered by many jewelers and appraisers. While not totally foolproof (recutting the diamond may affect Gemprint's reliability), it is playing an increasingly important role in the recovery and return of lost and stolen diamonds, and I recommend it where available.

Gemprint offers a fast and practical way to identify a diamond, even one already mounted, by capturing the image of the pattern of reflections created when the diamond is hit by a low-level laser beam. Depending upon the Gemprint system being used by the jeweler or appraiser, the image can be captured and stored on computer with digital imaging, or a photograph of the image may be taken. Each diamond produces a unique pattern, which is documented by this service. As with human fingerprints, no two gemprints are ever alike.

The process takes only a few minutes. The jeweler or appraiser will provide you with a certificate of registration that includes either a photograph or scanned image of the stone, along with other pertinent information about it. The information about your diamond is kept in the jeweler's or appraiser's file and is also transferred to Gemprint's international database, whereby interested law enforcement agencies can verify ownership of a diamond when recovered.

If your stone is ever lost or stolen, you or your insurer sends a notice-of-loss form to Gemprint, which will then notify appropriate law enforcement agencies. Police can then verify with the registry the identification of recovered diamonds, many of which are thereby returned to the rightful owners. As another safeguard, Gemprint also checks each new registration against its lost-and-stolen file before confirming and storing the registration. Gemprint can also be useful in checking a diamond that has been left for repair, cleaning, or resetting, to assure you that your stone has been returned.

Whether purchasing a diamond, or repairing, resizing, or remounting an heirloom, getting a Gemprint is another way to secure your investment. Increasingly, jewelers are offering Gemprint at no additional charge to customers making a diamond purchase. Whatever the case, the cost is nominal ($35 to $50) and may actually save you money in the long run since some insurance companies give 10 percent off the annual premium you pay if the diamond you are insuring has a Gemprint.

Gemprint is available in about 650 locations in the United States. For the location nearest you, contact Gemprint at 1-888-GEMPRINT.

Laser Inscriptions—Security and Romance

Laser inscription services are available at many gem-testing laboratories for a nominal charge. In the United States, laboratories offering inscription services include European Gemological Laboratory (EGL), International Gemmological Institute (IGI), Professional Gem Sciences (PGS), and the Gemological Institute of America (GIA); in Europe, EGL, Hoge Raad voor Diamant (HRD), and the Swiss Gemmological Institute (SSEF) (see appendix). Laser inscriptions can be useful in providing an identifying mark or a brand name, or to record the number of a corresponding laboratory report. Many companies selling branded diamonds now inscribe their own company logo and registration number for the particular stone on the girdle.

For the romantic, laser inscriptions also provide a way to add a secret, intimate message or to mark a special moment, occasion, or personal image of some type. The service can usually be completed within forty-eight hours, and the cost is usually under fifty dollars unless you have an unusually high number of characters or a complex image.

A romantic laser inscription

In addition to lasering, ion beam technology is being applied to the world of diamonds. International Gemmological Instititute will soon offer a new service that uses ion beam technology to mark a diamond in an innovative manner that is non-invasive, does not mar the diamond in any way, and is visible only with a special viewer. This new technology can also be used to apply a "brand" mark, thus making it more difficult to counterfeit branded diamonds. It will be more difficult to falsify or eradicate such marks as a result of the process itself, so this technology may ultimately replace laser inscriptions.

A Selected List of Recognized Laboratories

American Gemological
  Laboratories (AGL)
580 Fifth Avenue, Suite 706
New York, NY 10036

American Gem Trade Association
  Gemological Testing Center (AGTA)
18 East 48th St., Suite 1002
New York, NY 10017

CISGEM-External Service for
  Precious Stones
Via Ansperto, 5
20123 Milano
Italy

European Gemological
  Laboratory (EGL)
30 W. 47th St., Suite 205
New York, NY 10036

Gemmological Association and Gem
  Testing Laboratory of Great Britain
27 Greville St.
London EC1N 8SU
England

Gemological Association of All Japan
Katsumi Bldg., 5F, 5-25-8
Ueno, Taito-ku
Tokyo 110
Japan

Gem Certification and Appraisal Lab
580 Fifth Avenue, Suite 1205
New York, NY 10036

Gemological Institute of America
  (GIA) Gem Trade Laboratory (GTL)
580 Fifth Avenue
New York, NY 10036

Gemological Institute of America
  (GIA) Gem Trade Laboratory (GTL)
5345 Armada Dr.
Carlsbad, CA 92008

German Gemmological Laboratory
  (DSEF)
and Foundation for Gemstone Research
Prof.-Schlossmacher-Str. 1
D-55743 Idar-Oberstein
Germany

Gübelin Gemmological Lab
Maihofstrasse 102
CH-6006 Lucerne 9
Switzerland

Hoge Raad voor Diamant (HRD)
Hoveniersstraat, 22
B-2018 Antwerp
Belgium

International Gemmological Institute
579 Fifth Avenue
New York, NY 10017

Professional Gem Sciences (PGS)—

  5 South Wabash, Suite 1905
  Chicago, IL 60603

  550 South Hill St., Suite 1595
  Los Angeles, CA 90013

Swiss Gemmological Institute
SSEF—Schweizerische Stiftung für
  Edelstein-Forschung
Falknerstrasse 9
CH-4001 Basel
Switzerland

Selected Readings

Bronstein, Alan. *Forever Brilliant: The Aurora Collection of Colored Diamonds.* New York: Ashland Press, Inc., 2000. An excellent guide to the world of colored diamonds.

Bruton, E. *Diamonds.* 2nd ed. Radnor, Pa.: Chilton, 1978. An excellent, well-illustrated work for amateur and professional alike.

Hofer, Stephen C. *Collecting and Classifying Colored Diamonds.* New York: Ashland Press, 1998. A lavish, comprehensive work essential for anyone with a serious interest in the subject.

Koivula, John I. *The Microworld of Diamonds: A Visual Reference.* Northbrook, Ill.: Gemworld International, Inc., 2000. Presents an intriguing look at diamonds through the microscope in four hundred color photographs.

Matlins, Antoinette. *Colored Gemstones: The Antoinette Matlins Buying Guide—How to Select, Buy, Care for & Enjoy Sapphires, Emeralds, Rubies and Other Colored Gems with Confidence and Knowledge.* Woodstock, Vt.: GemStone Press, 2001. Covers every aspect of colored gemstones in detail, from their symbolic attributes to current frauds.

———. *Engagement & Wedding Rings: The Definitive Buying Guide for People in Love.* 2nd ed. Woodstock, Vt.: GemStone Press, 1999. Everything you need to know to select, design, buy, care for, and cherish your wedding or anniversary rings—his and hers. Beautiful photos of rings.

———. *The Pearl Book: The Definitive Buying Guide—How to Select, Buy, Care for & Enjoy Pearls.* 2nd ed. Woodstock, Vt.: GemStone Press, 1999. Covers every aspect of pearls, from lore and history to complete buying advice. An indispensable guide for the pearl lover.

Matlins, Antoinette, with Jill Newman. *Jewelry & Gems at Auction: The Definitive Guide to Buying & Selling at the Auction House & on Internet Auction Sites.* Woodstock, Vt.: GemStone Press, 2002. Everything anyone needs to know to buy gems and jewelry at auction.

Matlins, Antoinette L., and A. C. Bonanno. *Gem Identification Made Easy: A Hands-On Guide to More Confident Buying & Selling.* 2nd ed. Woodstock, Vt.: GemStone Press, 1997. A nontechnical book that makes gem identification possible for anyone. A "must" for beginners, and the experienced may pick up a few tips, too. Practical, easy to understand.

Pagel-Theisen, V. *Diamond Grading ABC.* 10th ed. New York: Rubin & Son, 1990. Highly recommended for anyone in diamond sales.

Roskin, Gary A. *Photo Masters for Diamond Grading.* Northbrook, Ill.: Gemworld International, Inc., 1994. A good reference with extraordinary photos for anyone interested in diamonds.

Color Plates and Exhibits

Charts

All the charts and the tables that appear here were especially designed and executed for use in this book; however, some from other publications were used as inspiration and reference. Grateful acknowledgment is given to the following for use of their charts as references:

The chart on page 67, "Sizes and Weights of Various Diamond Cuts," with permission of the Gemological Institute of America, from its book, *The Jewelers' Manual*.

The chart on page 68, "Diameters and Corresponding Weights of Round Brilliant-Cut Diamonds," with permission of the Gemological Institute of America, from its book *The Jewelers' Manual*.

The chart on page 110, "Comparison of Diamonds and Diamond Look-Alikes," with permission of the Gemological Institute of America, from its publication *Diamond Assignment No. 36*, page 27.

Black and White Photographs and Illustrations

Illustrations by Kathleen Robinson.

Page 27: EightStar® from EightStar Diamond Company (photo/Richard von Sternberg).

Page 29: Diamonds seen through viewer from EightStar Diamond Company (photo/Richard von Sternberg).

Page 33–34: Radiant and princess from Eugene Biro Corp.; Crisscut® from Christopher Designs (photo/Christony Inc.); Quadrillion™ from Ambar Diamonds; trilliant from MEFCO Inc. (photo/Sky Hall); Noble Cut™ from Doron Isaak; Gabrielle® from Suberi Brothers (photo/Peter Hurst); Spirit Sun® and Context® from Freiesleben; Lucida™ from Tiffany and Company (photo/Monica Stevenson); modern cushion-cut ring from Jonathan Birnbach for J. B. International; Royal Asscher® from Royal Asscher Diamond Company Ltd. (photo/Donald Barry Woodrow).

Page 36: Old Asscher from Jonathan Birnbach for J. B. International; old cushion from Antiquorum Auctioneers.

Page 37: Trapezoids and half-moons from Doron Isaak; briolette from Rough and Ready Gems (photo/Azad).

Page 59: Flawless and SI2 diamonds from Suberi Brothers.

Pages 135–137: Bezel-set rings by Robin Garin from Kwiat Couture; partial bezel-set ring from George Sawyer Design; five-stone bands from Lazare Kaplan, Inc.; heart-shaped diamond ring from Suberi Brothers; rings in gypsy and collet settings from Circle Round the Moon; channel-set baguette wedding band from JFA Designs; bar-set band (left) from Kwiat Couture; bar-set band (right) from J.B. International (photo/Peter Hurst); pavé rings from Barnett Robinson.

Page 172: "I Love You Sara" ring from European Gemological Laboratory.

Cover Photographs

Royal Asscher® from Royal Asscher Diamond Company Ltd. (photo/Donald Barry Woodrow); classic gem shapes (round, pear, heart, emerald-cut, oval and marquise) from Bellataire Diamonds, Inc.; Tiffany-style solitaire from Diamond Information Center; pear-shape diamond necklace from Bellataire Diamonds, Inc.; yellow radiant diamond ring from Jonathan Birnbach for J. B. International; diamond eternity band from J. B. International.

Color Photographs

I wish to thank the following persons and companies for the color photographs appearing in this new edition:

Page 1: Classic shapes from Bellataire Diamonds, Inc.

Page 2: Radiant from Eugene Biro Corp.; Gabrielle® rectangle and square from Suberi Brothers (photo/Peter Hurst); Crisscut® from Christopher Designs (photo/Christony Inc.); Royal Asscher® from Royal Asscher Diamond Company Ltd. (photo/Donald Barry Woodrow); Quadrillion™ from Ambar Diamonds; Lucida™ from Tiffany and Company (photo/Monica Stevenson); Context® from Freiesleben.

Page 3: Gabrielle® round and heart from Suberi Brothers (photo/Peter Hurst); Spirit Sun® from Freiesleben; EightStar® from EightStar Diamond Company (photo/Richard von Sternberg); trilliant from Eugene Biro Corp.; Lily Cut® from Lili Diamonds (design/Siman-Tov Brothers); briolette and rondelles from Manak Jewels, Inc.; earrings, half-moons, and trapezoids from Doron Isaak; Crisscut® baguettes from Christopher Designs (photo/Christony Inc.).

Page 4: Fancy diamond "peacock," blue and pink diamonds, and green diamonds from Robert Haack Diamonds (photos/Sky Hall); fancy-color diamond floral brooch from Sotheby's, NY; assorted natural-color diamond suite from Aurora Gems Inc. (photo/Tino Hammid).

Page 5: Brooch from Rudolf Friedmann; black diamond rings from Manak Jewels, Inc.; green diamond rings from Etienne Perret; necklace from NOVA by Gruber; Attia Collection from Eli Jewels.

Page 6 and 7: All jewelry from designers listed. (Kwiat Couture by Robin Garin © 2001; Gabrielle jewelry from Suberi Brothers.)

Page 8: Ring and necklace (top left) from Bellataire Diamonds, Inc.; bracelet (top right) from NOVA by Gruber; Mark Michael jewelry designed and manufactured by Mark Michael Designs (photo/JQ Magazine); Doron Isaak jewelry from Doron Isaak.

Page 9: Necklace (top left) from Christopher Designs (photo/Christony Inc.); necklace (right) from James Breski; three rings (top) and bracelet (middle) from Barnett Robinson; Scott Keating rings from Scott Keating Design; Jean-François Albert ring from Designs by Jean-François Albert.

Page 10: Three-stone rings: top, from private collection of David and Agnes Sarns (design/Carvin French and Antoinette Matlins; photo/Tibor Ardai); middle right and left, from Jonathan Birnbach for J. B. International; bottom, from Fullcut. Classic solitaires: left and right, from Lazare Kaplan International; bottom (Tiffany-style), from the Diamond Information Service. Ring with tiny channel-set stones from a private collector (design/Carvin French and Antoinette Matlins; photo/Tibor Ardai). Classic round (with tapered baguettes), yellow radiant, and oval (with tapered baguettes) rings from Jonathan Birnbach for J. B. International. Heirloom reproductions: left, from Mark Silverstein for Varna; right, from Richard Kimball. Rare vivid yellow emerald-cut ring from Antiquorum Auctioneers.

Page 11: Top left, from Designs by Jean-François Albert; top middle and right, from Alex Primak; middle left, Nina Collection by H. Stern Jewellers Inc.; middle right (single band), from J. B. International (photo/Peter Hurst); middle right (two bands), from Kwiat, Inc. (photo/David R. Kaplan, © 2001); bottom left, from Kwiat Couture; bottom right, from Scott Keating Design.

Page 12: Luminari™ and Ultimate Created Diamonds™ from Lucent Diamonds (photos/Tino Hammid).

Index

The "Unofficial Bible" for the Gem & Jewelry Buyer

JEWELRY & GEMS:
THE BUYING GUIDE, 5TH EDITION

NEW Retail Price Guides

How to Buy Diamonds, Pearls, Colored Gemstones, Gold & Jewelry with Confidence and Knowledge

by Antoinette Matlins, P.G., *and* A. C. Bonanno, F.G.A., P.G., A.S.A.

—over 250,000 copies in print—

Learn the tricks of the trade from *insiders:* How to buy diamonds, pearls, precious and other popular colored gems with confidence and knowledge. More than just a buying guide . . . discover what's available and what choices you have, what determines quality as well as cost, what questions to ask before you buy and what to get in writing. Easy to read and understand. Excellent for staff training.

6" x 9", 320 pp., 16 full-color pages & over 200 color and b/w illustrations and photos; index

Quality Paperback, ISBN 0-943763-31-2 **$18.95**

Hardcover, ISBN 0-943763-30-4 **$24.95**

• COMPREHENSIVE • EASY TO READ • PRACTICAL •

ENGAGEMENT & WEDDING RINGS, 2ND EDITION

by Antoinette Matlins, P.G., *and* A. C. Bonanno, F.G.A., A.S.A., M.G.A.

Tells **everything you need to know to design, select, buy and enjoy that "perfect" ring** and to truly experience the wonder and excitement that should be part of it.

Updated, expanded, filled with valuable information.

Engagement & Wedding Rings, 2nd Ed., will help you make the *right* choice. You will discover romantic traditions behind engagement and wedding rings, how to select the right style and design for *you,* tricks to get what you want on a budget, ways to add new life to an "heirloom," what to do to protect yourself against fraud, and much more.

Dazzling 16-page color section of rings showing antique to contemporary designs.

Over 400 illustrations and photographs. Index.

6" x 9", 304 pp., Quality Paperback, ISBN 0-943763-20-7 **$16.95**

JEWELRY & GEMS AT AUCTION

The Definitive Guide to Buying & Selling at the Auction House & on Internet Auction Sites

by Antoinette Matlins, P.G.

with contributions by Jill Newman

As buying and selling at auctions—both traditional auction houses and "virtual" Internet auctions—moves into the mainstream, **consumers need to know how to "play the game."** There are treasures to be had and money to be saved and made, but buying and selling at auction offers unique risks as well as unique opportunities. This book makes available—for the first time—detailed information on how to buy and sell jewelry and gems at auction without making costly mistakes.

6" x 9", 352 pp., fully illustrated

Quality Paperback Original, ISBN 0-943763-29-0 **$19.95**

Now You Can Have the "Professional's Advantage"!
With Your OWN Jeweler's Loupe—
The Essential "TOOL OF THE TRADE"!

Personally selected by the authors, this valuable jeweler's aid is *now available to the consumer* from GemStone Press. And GemStone Press includes, FREE, a copy of "The Professional's Advantage: How to Use the Loupe and What to Look For," a $5.00 value, written with the jewelry buyer in mind. You can now *have more fun while shopping and make your choice with greater confidence*. This is not just a magnifying glass. It is specially made to be used to examine jewelry. It will help you to—

- *Enjoy* the inner beauty of the gem as well as the outer beauty.
- *Protect yourself*—see scratches, chips, or cracks that reduce the value of a stone or make it vulnerable to greater damage.
- *Prevent loss*—spot weak prongs that may break and cause the stone to fall from the setting.
- *Avoid bad cutting*, poor proportioning and poor symmetry.
- *Identify the telltale signs* of glass or imitation.
- . . . And much more, as revealed in "The Professional's Advantage"!

You'll love it. You'll enjoy looking at gems and jewelry up close—it makes this special experience even more exciting. And sometimes, as one of our readers recently wrote:

"Just having the loupe and looking like I knew how to use it changed the way I was treated."

CALL NOW AND WE'LL RUSH THE LOUPE TO YOU.
FOR TOLL FREE CREDIT CARD ORDERS:
800-962-4544

Item	Quantity	Price Each	TOTAL
Standard 10X Triplet Loupe	_____	$29.00	= $_____
Bausch & Lomb 10X Triplet Loupe	_____	$44.00	= $_____
"The Professional's Advantage" Booklet	1 per Loupe	$ 5.00	= Free
Insurance/Packing/Shipping in the U.S.*	1st Loupe	$ 4.95	= $ 4.95
*Outside U.S.: Specify shipping method (insured) and provide a credit card number for payment.	Each add'l	$ 3.00	= $_____

TOTAL: $_____

Check enclosed for $_____ (Payable to: GEMSTONE PRESS)
Charge my credit card: ❏ Visa ❏ MasterCard
Name on Card _____
Cardholder Address: Street _____
City/State/Zip _____
Credit Card # _____ Exp. Date _____
Signature _____ Phone (____)_____
Please send to: ❏ Same as Above ❏ Address Below
Name _____
Street _____
City/State/Zip _____ Phone (____)_____

Phone, mail, fax, or e-mail orders to: GEMSTONE PRESS, Sunset Farm Offices, Rte. 4,
P.O. Box 237, Woodstock, VT 05091 • *Tel:* (802) 457-4000 • *Fax:* (802) 457-4004
Credit Card Orders: (800) 962-4544 • **www.gemstonepress.com**
Generous Discounts on Quantity Orders

TOTAL SATISFACTION GUARANTEE
If for any reason you're not completely delighted with your purchase, return it in resellable condition within 30 days for a full refund.

Prices subject to change

016

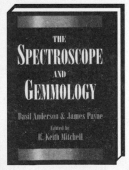

Buy Your *"Tools of the Trade..."*

Gem Identification Instruments directly from *GemStone Press*

Whatever instrument you need, GemStone Press can help.
Use our convenient order form, or contact us directly for assistance.

ITEM / QUANTITY	PRICE EA.*	TOTAL $
Lamps—Ultraviolet & High Intensity		
_____ Small LW/SW (UVP)	$71.00	_____
_____ Large LW/SW (UVP)	$189.00	_____
_____ Viewing Cabinet for Large Lamp (UVP)	$147.00	_____
_____ **Purchase Large Lamp & Cabinet together for $299 and save $37.00**	$299.00	_____
_____ Dialite Flip Lamp (Eickhorst)	$64.95	_____
Other Light Sources		
_____ Large Maglite	$15.00	_____
_____ Flex Light	$29.95	_____
Refractometers		
_____ Standard Refractometer (Eickhorst)	$625.00	_____
_____ Pocket Refractometer (Eickhorst)	$495.00	_____
_____ Refractive Index Liquid—10 gram	$42.50	_____
Spectroscopes		
_____ Spectroscope—Pocket-sized model (OPL)	$89.00	_____
_____ Spectroscope—Desk model w/stand (OPL)	$225.00	_____

Shipping/Insurance per order in the U.S.: $4.95 first item, $3.00 each add'l item; $7.95 total for pocket instrument set. SHIPPING/INS. $ _____

Outside the U.S.: Please specify *insured* shipping method you prefer and provide a credit card number for payment. **TOTAL $ _____** **

Check enclosed for $ _____ (Payable to: GEMSTONE PRESS)

Charge my credit card: ❏ Visa ❏ MasterCard

Name on Card _____

Cardholder Address: Street _____

City/State/Zip _____

Credit Card # _____ Exp. Date _____

Signature _____ Phone (____)_____

Please send to: ❏ Same as Above ❏ Address Below

Name _____

Street _____

City/State/Zip _____ Phone (____)_____

Phone, mail, fax, or e-mail orders to:

GEMSTONE PRESS, P.O. Box 237, Woodstock, VT 05091

Tel: **(802) 457-4000** • *Fax:* **(802) 457-4004** • *Credit Card Orders:* **(800) 962-4544**

www.gemstonepress.com

Generous Discounts on Quantity Orders

Cut along dotted line

See Over for More Instruments

TOTAL SATISFACTION GUARANTEE
If for any reason you're not completely delighted with your purchase, return it in resellable condition within 30 days for a full refund.

*Prices, manufacturing specifications, and terms subject to change without notice. Orders accepted subject to availability.

**All orders must be prepaid by credit card, money order or check in U.S. funds drawn on a U.S. bank.

016

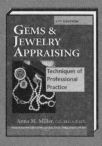

Please send me:

CAMEOS OLD & NEW, 2ND EDITION
_____ copies at $19.95 (Quality Paperback) *plus s/h**

COLORED GEMSTONES: THE ANTOINETTE MATLINS BUYING GUIDE
_____ copies at $16.95 (Quality Paperback) *plus s/h**

DIAMONDS: THE ANTOINETTE MATLINS BUYING GUIDE
_____ copies at $16.95 (Quality Paperback) *plus s/h**

ENGAGEMENT & WEDDING RINGS: THE DEFINITIVE BUYING GUIDE, 2ND EDITION
_____ copies at $16.95 (Quality Paperback) *plus s/h**

**GEM IDENTIFICATION MADE EASY, 2ND EDITION:
A HANDS-ON GUIDE TO MORE CONFIDENT BUYING & SELLING**
_____ copies at $34.95 (Hardcover) *plus s/h**

GEMS & JEWELRY APPRAISING, 2ND EDITION
_____ copies at $39.95 (Hardcover) *plus s/h**

ILLUSTRATED GUIDE TO JEWELRY APPRAISING, 2ND EDITION
_____ copies at $39.95 (Hardcover) *plus s/h**

**JEWELRY & GEMS AT AUCTION: THE DEFINITIVE GUIDE TO BUYING & SELLING
AT THE AUCTION HOUSE & ON INTERNET AUCTION SITES**
_____ copies at $19.95 (Quality Paperback) *plus s/h**

JEWELRY & GEMS: THE BUYING GUIDE, 5TH EDITION
_____ copies at $18.95 (Quality Paperback) *plus s/h**
_____ copies at $24.95 (Hardcover) *plus s/h**

THE PEARL BOOK, 2ND EDITION: THE DEFINITIVE BUYING GUIDE
_____ copies at $19.95 (Quality Paperback) *plus s/h**

THE SPECTROSCOPE AND GEMMOLOGY
_____ copies at $60.00 (Hardcover) *plus s/h**

**TREASURE HUNTER'S GEM & MINERAL GUIDES TO THE U.S.A.:
WHERE & HOW TO DIG, PAN AND MINE YOUR OWN GEMS & MINERALS—
IN 4 REGIONAL VOLUMES** $14.95 per copy (Quality Paperback) *plus s/h**
_____ copies of NE States _____ copies of SE States _____ copies of NW States _____ copies of SW States

* In U.S.: Shipping/Handling: $3.75 for 1st book, $2.00 each additional book.
  Outside U.S.: Specify shipping method (insured) and provide a credit card number for payment.

- -

Check enclosed for $_____ (Payable to: GEMSTONE Press)
Charge my credit card: ❏ Visa ❏ MasterCard
Name on Card (PRINT) _____
Cardholder Address: Street _____
City/State/Zip _____
Credit Card # _____ Exp. Date _____
Signature _____ Phone (_____)_____
Please send to: ❏ Same as Above ❏ Address Below
Name (PRINT) _____
Street _____
City/State/Zip _____ Phone (_____)_____

Phone, mail, fax, or e-mail orders to:
GEMSTONE PRESS, Sunset Farm Offices,
Rte. 4, P.O. Box 237, Woodstock, VT 05091
Tel: (802) 457-4000 • *Fax:* (802) 457-4004
Credit Card Orders: (800) 962-4544
www.gemstonepress.com
Generous Discounts on Quantity Orders

Prices subject
to change

Try Your Bookstore First